SOFTWA
DEVELOF

BCS, THE CHARTERED INSTITUTE FOR IT

BCS, The Chartered Institute for IT, is committed to making IT good for society. We use the power of our network to bring about positive, tangible change. We champion the global IT profession and the interests of individuals, engaged in that profession, for the benefit of all.

Exchanging IT expertise and knowledge
The Institute fosters links between experts from industry, academia and business to promote new thinking, education and knowledge sharing.

Supporting practitioners
Through continuing professional development and a series of respected IT qualifications, the Institute seeks to promote professional practice tuned to the demands of business. It provides practical support and information services to its members and volunteer communities around the world.

Setting standards and frameworks
The Institute collaborates with government, industry and relevant bodies to establish good working practices, codes of conduct, skills frameworks and common standards. It also offers a range of consultancy services to employers to help them adopt best practice.

Become a member
Over 70,000 people including students, teachers, professionals and practitioners enjoy the benefits of BCS membership. These include access to an international community, invitations to a roster of local and national events, career development tools and a quarterly thought-leadership magazine. Visit www.bcs.org/membership to find out more.

Further information
BCS, The Chartered Institute for IT,
First Floor, Block D,
North Star House, North Star Avenue,
Swindon, SN2 1FA, United Kingdom.
T +44 (0) 1793 417 417
(Monday to Friday, 09:00 to 17:00 UK time)
www.bcs.org/contact
http://shop.bcs.org/

SOFTWARE
DEVELOPER

Jill Clarke

The
Chartered
Institute
for IT

Published by BCS Learning and Development Ltd, a wholly owned subsidiary of BCS, The Chartered Institute for IT, First Floor, Block D, North Star House, North Star Avenue, Swindon, SN2 1FA, UK.
www.bcs.org

Paperback ISBN: 978-1-78017-501-0
PDF ISBN: 978-1-78017-502-7
ePUB ISBN: 978-1-78017-503-4
Kindle ISBN: 978-1-78017-504-1

Ebook available

British Cataloguing in Publication Data.
A CIP catalogue record for this book is available at the British Library.

Disclaimer:
The views expressed in this book are of the authors and do not necessarily reflect the views of the Institute or BCS Learning and Development Ltd except where explicitly stated as such. Although every care has been taken by the authors and BCS Learning and Development Ltd in the preparation of the publication, no warranty is given by the authors or BCS Learning and Development Ltd as publisher as to the accuracy or completeness of the information contained within it and neither the authors nor BCS Learning and Development Ltd shall be responsible or liable for any loss or damage whatsoever arising by virtue of such information or any instructions or advice contained within this publication or by any of the aforementioned.

Publisher's acknowledgements
Reviewers: Mark Berthelemy, Stephen Mariadas and James Millar
Publisher: Ian Borthwick
Commissioning editor: Rebecca Youé
Production manager: Florence Leroy
Project manager: Sunrise Setting Ltd
Copy-editor: Gillian Bourn
Proofreader: Sarah Cook
Indexer: Matthew Gale
Cover design: Alex Wright
Cover image: istock/RandyHume
Typeset by Lapiz Digital Services, Chennai, India

CONTENTS

LIST OF FIGURES AND TABLES

ABOUT THE AUTHOR

Jill Clarke is an experienced freelance developer and enthusiastic trainer of the existing and next generation of software developers. Her initial roles as a Cobol programmer laid the foundations for a working life programming many different systems in a variety of industries using many different programming languages.

She runs her own company (Bear Computer Services Ltd) where currently much of the work she does is in training developers (via JBI Training) at many well-known companies both large and small in new languages, methodologies (she is a professional Scrum Master), techniques and tools in traditional software development as well as the ever expanding web development sector. She still loves working as a developer and does development work for both enjoyment and profit as well as to keep her skills fresh and up to date.

She is a member of BCS and in her spare time she volunteers on the BCS Women committee and can also occasionally be found volunteering at The National Museum of Computing (based at Bletchley Park) where she developed the Software Gallery along with Bob Jones. She was runner up in the BCS IT Trainer of the year award in 2007 and is a Fellow of the Learning and Performance Institute.

ACKNOWLEDGEMENTS

Starting at the beginning, I would like to express my love and gratitude to my brother and parents (Vern and Beryl) who always encouraged me in this career (and in life) even though programming was a less popular career choice in the 1970s when I first sat an aptitude exam.

From my early days as a junior programmer I'd like to thank my first mentor (John Wright) who helped me when I was working in Birmingham and all the many people since who have helped, inspired and supported me in my career. The developer community is rich with these types of people; find a company and role where you can benefit from and contribute to this supportive atmosphere.

For the book I'd like to thank Ian Borthwick and Rebecca Youé who approached me about writing it. The people who contributed to the case study chapter all gave freely of their time and experiences, they were enthusiastic and honest and bring the subject matter to life, thank you:

Jeremy Clarke
Emma Bostian
Chris Ashton
Eva Dovc
Simon Kemp
Zara Ahmed

I'd also like to thank Jon Bambaji and the team (Mervyn, Pavlos, Nigel and Bill) at JBI Training who cleared time in my schedule so I could write the book.

ABBREVIATIONS

AI	artificial intelligence
API	application programming interface
ATM	automated teller machine
BCS	BCS, The Chartered Institute for IT
BDD	behaviour driven development
BIOS	basic input/output system
CASE	computer aided software engineering
CAST	computer aided software testing
CI	continuous integration
CPD	continuing professional development
CPU	central processor unit
CSS	cascading style sheets
DBMS	database management system
DRY	don't repeat yourself
EDI	electronic data interchange
ERD	entity relationship diagram
ERM	entity relationship modelling
FTP	file transfer protocol
GDPR	General Data Protection Regulation
GPS	global positioning system
HP	Hewlett Packard
HTML	Hyper Text Markup Language
IDE	integrated development environment
IoT	internet of things

JSON	JavaScript Object Notation
MoSCoW	must have, should have, could have, won't have this time
MVC	model view controller
NFR	non-functional requirements
OOP	object oriented programming
OWASP	Open Web Application Security Project
PC	personal computer
PHP	(originally) personal home page
PRINCE2	Projects IN Controlled Environments
ROI	return on investment
SDLC	software (or systems) development life cycle
SFIA	Skills Framework for the Information Age
SQL	Structured Query Language
SSADM	structured systems analysis design method
STEM	science, technology, engineering, mathematics
TDD	test driven development
TL;DR	too long; didn't read
UML	Unified Modelling Language
URL	uniform resource locator
UX	user experience
XML	eXtensible Markup Language

GLOSSARY

Agile: an umbrella term for a particular set of frameworks and practices used during product development

Anti-patterns: bad practices in code development, see also code smells

Applications (Apps): programs that run on a computer or electronic device. Apps that can be downloaded for a mobile phone via an app store are known as 'native apps' because they run on a particular mobile platform, for example Android or iOS

Attribute: (in databases) a data element (field) associated with an entity, for example a customer number, customer name, customer address or current balance

Behaviour driven development (BDD): a top-down development approach where the user goals and product behaviour are defined collaboratively

Blockchain: a system where the transactions made using an electronic currency (for example BitCoin) are logged

Continuous integration (CI): a development practice where small pieces of work are submitted frequently to a shared repository containing the most up-to-date version of a product

Class (object oriented terminology): a template for something used in your system, for example an order

Code smells: bad practices that may be used when writing code, see also anti-patterns

Data dictionary: a list of data items with descriptions of their data type and use in the system

Database: a collection of logically related data that can be defined and controlled independently of user applications. They are made up of tables (for example 'Customers' or 'Accounts') which consist of rows (typically one row for each customer or account) which are, in turn, made up of columns (each of which is a piece of data related to the row)

Database management system (DBMS): the software used for developing and managing a database independently of any programs that use the data

Deployment: the stage in product development when you ship the product to the customer

DRY: don't repeat yourself, a development principle which helps avoid duplicated logic by having one procedure which can be called by other procedures; in other words, a piece of reusable code

Encapsulation: (object oriented terminology) the concept of an object containing its data and the methods that can be used to read or change that data

Entity: (in databases) something which an organisation collects and stores data on, for example a customer, an order or a bank account

Entity relationship diagram (ERD): the diagram part of an ERM

Entity relationship model (ERM): a mixture of diagrams and text description which describe data usually held in a database

False feature rich: in simple terms, this means giving the user more than they asked for in the way of software or webpage functionality

Global positioning system (GPS): a way of determining your location on the planet

Global variables: variables are the yellow sticky notes of the programming world, they hold data temporarily for use at a later time in your code, then they can be thrown away. A global variable is one that can be used anywhere in your program

Identifier: (in databases) an entity has an identifier, that is, an attribute that uniquely identifies an occurrence of a particular entity among many occurrences of the same entity; for example the identifier for a customer might be Customer Number. An identifier is sometimes called a Primary Key

Inheritance: (object oriented terminology) an object can use (inherits) the methods and properties defined by its class

Instance: (object oriented terminology) a copy of a class; an instance of a class is called an object

Internet of things (IoT): a system of interrelated or interconnected electronic computer devices; for example, the ability to control your home heating with an app on your phone

JSON: a simple data-interchange format, often used when sending data across the internet

Method: (object oriented terminology) something that can be done by an object (a piece of functionality); for example, you can Place an Order (Place is the method, Order is the object)

Modules: sections or parts of code

Normalisation: (in database design) a set of rules and guidelines that help you create well-designed databases

Object: (object oriented terminology) an instance of a defined class, for example the Order object, when you place an order the system will create an order object in the code to represent your particular order

Pair programming: a technique where two people work/ collaborate on the same piece of code

Patterns: (in code or development) good practice, tried and tested ways of developing code in order to solve a particular problem

Property: (object oriented terminology) a piece of data relating to an object

Refactoring: the name given to rewriting a piece of code in order to improve the quality, readability or maintainability of that code

Relationship: (in databases) the term used for the association between entities, for example a customer is related to an order by the relationship 'places'

Robust code: software that is written in such a way that it does not break easily when errors occur

Scrum: a methodology used to implement Agile practices during product development

Software or systems development life cycle (SDLC): the lifetime of a product/system, from conception to eventual decommissioning

SQL: Structured Query Language, a language used to access data from a database

Stakeholders: people (or sometimes other systems or groups) that have an interest in a product's development

Syntactic sugar: a phrase often used about a development libraries capabilities; it refers to the fact that the library provides an easy to use way of doing something. It hides the underlying difficulties of a language or process

Technical debt: the term used when refactoring is identified as necessary but not carried out

Test driven development (TDD): a technique where tests are created at the same time (before) the code that they test

UML: Unified Modelling Language, a set of modelling techniques which are grouped together under one title. They can be used to diagrammatically represent a system

URL: Uniform Resource Locator, an address on the internet

Use cases: used to describe what a system does from the standpoint of an external observer, in development this is used to work out what the boundaries of a system are, what is included and what is excluded

User stories: a technique used widely in modern software development methodologies such as Agile/Scrum. They are simple-to-read definitions of a user's goal for a product

Waterfall: a model which shows a traditional (older style) software development life cycle

PREFACE

When I first started writing code we were simply known as programmers. The roles in my first work experience as a programmer were well defined:

1. The analyst analysed the problem.

2. The designer designed the solution.

3. The programmer wrote the code (by hand, on COBOL coding sheets) and then wrote the Job Control Request sheet to define what needed running and how.

4. The punch operator transferred the code onto punched cards.

5. These were passed to the operator who ran the code on the big old mainframe.

6. Some days later, the programmer was given a (memory) core dump with error listing, they worked out what was wrong and wrote out the corrections, which went to the punch card operator etc.

Try transferring that process to modern text messaging:

1. Someone asks what you want to say and who you want to say it to.

2. Someone else works out the right words and emojis.

3. You write that on a piece of squared paper (one character per square).

4. Someone else transfers that to the correct text message request form.

5. Someone else types that into the mobile phone (that is shared by the whole office).

6. You then get a printed reply to your text.

It doesn't even bear thinking about nowadays, thank goodness for progress.

Today even the job title is different. Modern terminology tends to use the term 'developer' as opposed to 'programmer', although the terms are used interchangeably too. The modern role of software developer is very different from that first work experience, and thankfully much broader, more interesting and dynamic too. This book explores this modern role which now has as many dimensions as names within the modern workplace.

No previous knowledge is assumed so the book will be suitable for anyone who is either looking to find out more about the role, just starting out in their career in the IT industry, or looking to further develop self-taught programming skills.

This book will cover what the role is and the types of skills and tools commonly needed to do the role; it will also look at the different relevant applications, environments and industry sectors, giving examples of popular programming languages or associated techniques along the way.

SYMBOLS USED IN THE BOOK

 Side track

 Thinking moment

1   INTRODUCTION

> It's the only job I can think of where I get to be both an
> engineer and an artist. There's an incredible, rigorous,
> technical element to it, which I like because you have
> to do very precise thinking. On the other hand, it has a
> wildly creative side where the boundaries of imagination
> are the only real limitation.
>
>   Andy Hertzfeld, talking about programming

This book will cover the role of software developer in the
modern workplace. It will look at generally accepted skills,
behaviours, practices and competencies commonly used in
the industry for the role.

While reading this book you should bear in mind that the role
of developer is not exactly the same for every organisation,
sector or even department that employs people with the job
title of developer. The skills you need and the work you do
will always be context-dependent based on the organisation,
sector, product, environment and programming language
applicable to you.

This chapter will introduce you to all the various titles that
could be used to refer to someone who writes code. It will
also introduce the broad range of skills and competencies
that could be needed for the role. When you look at a software
developer role you will need a mix of these different skills
depending on the particular role you apply for.

A ROSE BY ANY OTHER NAME – PROGRAMMER, DEVELOPER, SOFTWARE ENGINEER, APP BUILDER, CODER

First of all, let's clarify the job title itself; do you want to be a
programmer, developer, software engineer, application (app)
builder or coder? Why are there different terms and what is
the difference between them?

Programmer

Programmer, a person who programs computers. As well as the laptop and desktop computers we often use, modern life has embedded 'computers' (or microprocessors) in many products from mobile phones to washing machines. The term 'programmer' is a general term for anyone who programs computers; this means that all the other people fulfilling the roles described below can also be described as programmers.

Developer

Developer, a person who develops programs for computers or other devices. This role generally covers tasks in addition to writing code, for example, there may be a need for some design and testing and other associated skills. Quite often the role has an additional descriptor, for example 'web developer' (a person who creates webpages and systems that run across the internet).

Software engineer

Initially the people who programmed computers were programmers; Margaret Hamilton, who coined the term 'software engineering', said she used it to get across to people the fact that programming was a skill in the development of technology in just the same way as electrical or hardware engineering was.

Now, in some companies (and countries) the difference between the terms software engineer and programmer or developer is the level of academic achievement gained – there are degrees in software engineering.

Software engineers are perceived as people who not only create programs but use formal processes and techniques to best design and develop that software.

App builder

Apps is an abbreviation most commonly used for programs that run on mobile devices such as phones and tablets, although recently it is also being used for software running on a PC. App builders (or app developers) are the people who create these programs.

Coder

The simplest of all the titles, a coder is someone who writes code, so all of the above job titles are filled by coders.

So, which one to use?

These terms are a cause of some debate and discussion within the industry. Modern terminology often uses the term developers instead of programmers (particularly in relation to things like DevOps – covered later in this book) and I have recently seen social media discussions (and heated debates) where people perceive elitism in one term or another.

All of these roles can be considered programmers broadly, because in all of these roles you write code and produce varying types of software, for example applications, mobile apps, games or webpages. This book focuses on the more modern term 'software developer'.

The terminology takes into account the practices, platforms and competencies of the person who writes the code and the depth of their participation in the process.

The important detail is not really what you are called but what you do in your production of software, your ability to use the correct techniques and practices to create well-designed, functioning, maintainable, efficient code.

Whether you learn those skills 'up front', 'on the job' or 'too late to be of use' depends very much on the individual, the company, the environment and the product.

SKILLS AND COMPETENCIES, FRAME OF REFERENCE

Because the software developer role can cover so many different types of product, from developing operating systems such as Microsoft Windows, iOS or Linux; developing a game to run on a popular games console, through to developing an ecommerce site for a retail outlet, it is useful to have a frame of reference for professional skills, standards and competencies. Some of these skills and competencies will have more emphasis in some business sectors than others. This book will use SFIA (Skills Framework for the Information Age) as that frame of reference, and will be introducing different aspects of the related professional skills and competencies plus associated areas.

See SFIA online for more detail:
https://www.sfia-online.org/en

Tempting as it is to think that all a developer needs is knowledge of a programming language, that is not the case, there are many more aspects that are required for the developer to be capable of fulfilling the role. Figure 1.1 is from the SFIA website and shows the balance of skills and technical knowledge in the context of an IT role.

In Figure 1.1, the professional skills and knowledge are what you know, while the behaviours are how you use those skills or that knowledge, for example in influencing or managing.

Professional skills cover such things as knowing a programming language; tools include the applications you need to use to enter the language into the computer. Methodologies are the set of methods, principles or activities you use to accomplish something, for example, a Scrum methodology is often used to help us manage software development. The context is the understanding of the business or industry sector. The SFIA framework also highlights the behaviours required; that is, in

Figure 1.1 Context for the different aspects that contribute to capability (Source: Reproduced with permission of SFIA Foundation)

this case, the communication and interpersonal skills, all of which need to be understood in context.

The central concept is experience. If you have been looking for a role as a developer you will often see requirements such as 'must have 5 years' experience' (frustratingly sometimes in things that have only been out for 3 years!). The reason experience is so valued is because it shows you can correctly apply your skills; the more you practise the skills the better you become at them.

Released in 2015, version 6 of the SFIA Framework (https://www.sfia-online.org/en/framework/sfia-6) gives the following description of general professional skills for a software developer:

> The design, creation, testing and documenting of new and amended software components from supplied specifications in accordance with agreed development and security standards and processes.

Released just 3 years later in 2018, and ably illustrating the dynamic nature and needs of the industry, SFIA version 7 (SFIA, 2019) suggests a broader range of skills and competencies for that same role:

> The planning, designing, creation, amending, verification, testing and documentation of new and amended software components in order to deliver agreed value to stakeholders. The identification, creation and application of agreed software development and security standards and processes. Adopting and adapting software development life cycle models based on the context of the work and selecting appropriately from predictive (plan-driven) approaches or adaptive (iterative/agile) approaches.

This book is designed to give you an introduction to the areas mentioned in these skills lists. It will not cover every aspect of every skill but it will give simple examples and pointers where possible to further reading and study.

SUMMARY

This chapter explained the varying job titles related to the role of software developer; it also cited SFIA as the frame of reference for the skills and competencies that will be covered in this book.

This chapter has covered 'who', the following chapters cover the remaining key points for developers:

What, Why, When, How, Where and Who are the six honest serving men from the poem that follows Rudyard Kipling's (1900) story *The Elephant's Child.*

'I KEEP six honest serving-men

(They taught me all I knew);

Their names are What and Why and When

And How and Where and Who.'

2 OVERVIEW OF SOFTWARE DEVELOPMENT IN CONTEXT

The trouble with programmers is that you can never tell what a programmer is doing until it's too late.

Seymour Cray

The SFIA framework specifically mentions context, so this chapter is a broad introduction to the practice of software development and where the developer role belongs in the greater context of systems and solution development. It considers what a developer produces and examines the broad range of products and industries that need developers. It also looks at where development output and developers fit into a system life cycle (that is, the lifetime of a product/system, from conception to eventual decommissioning).

WHAT IS DEVELOPMENT?

In the context of this book I am using 'development' to mean the creation of a program or part of a program, intended to run on a computer or other electronic device. Rather than saying all that every time, I will simply refer to what a developer produces as a product or program.

THE BUSINESS CONTEXT

The role of developer requires a set of skills, used across a very wide and varied range of businesses, sectors and industries. Developers produce a wide range of products; these can be platform- (what type of system it runs on), sector- (what type of industry it is used in) or use- (what its intended purpose is) specific.

In the SFIA framework the role of software developer belongs in a group of roles entitled 'systems development'; on the skills webpage at the time of writing, systems development belongs in the solution development and implementation category.

Let's consider the terms 'systems development' and 'solution development' for a moment. A system is defined as a set of things working together as part of a complex whole; in an IT context, systems development is the process of creating (analysing, designing, building, testing and implementing) a new software application or program. A solution is a means of dealing with a problem and in the business context, when you undertake solution development you are trying to provide something that will fulfil a need (or perceived need) or resolve a problem. These two terms, 'solution' and 'system' help us to understand why we develop software; we have a business problem and software systems provide the solution (or part of the solution) to that problem.

That problem or need could be any number of things; some example problems with potential solutions could include:

- Problem – delivering medication to patients takes up a disproportionate amount of time for nursing staff; these highly trained individuals could be better utilised in doing other things.

- Solution – a means of automating medication delivery for the health centre.

- Problem – people who post images to a social media site do not always post appropriate images.

- Solution – a social media platform with AI-based image filtering.

A developer could create part or all of the system that provides the solution to these problems or needs.

APPLICATIONS, APPS, WEBSITES, EMBEDDED SOFTWARE, OPERATING SYSTEMS

In the previous chapter I mentioned some of the types of software a developer may create, such as operating systems, applications, mobile apps, games and websites. The type of software you develop is dependent on the type of business or industry sector you are working in. Let's look at that in a little more detail.

Systems programming

This tends to be a more specialised type of software development where developers create operating systems and software that controls the general running of a system. This type of software tends to interface with hardware or other pieces of software by providing services, for example writing to a hard disk or printing capability. Examples of this type of software include Microsoft Windows, Apple's iOS, Android and Linux. End users can access the capabilities of this type of software via applications that have been written to use the interfaces made available by the system software. Examples of applications that use the capabilities of the system's software include Microsoft's Windows Explorer and Apple's Finder, both of which give the end user access to the file system which is managed by their respective operating system.

Companies that employ developers to write this type of software tend to be specialist IT or computer-focused industries, the majority of which will be large companies or organisations.

To work as a developer in this area you will generally need a good understanding of hardware and how hardware and software interact, plus an understanding of file systems and interfaces for input/output and data exchange. Working in this area you would be more likely to have formal degree-level education in hardware, software and systems engineering.

Enterprise programming

This type of software is written with a business or organisation in mind; it is designed to help run the business or organisation or to support the business goals. This type of software tends to be aimed at large businesses, sectors or organisations such as government or education.

The type of product created in enterprise programming targets areas such as accounting, payroll, human resources and project management. There are many other types of enterprise software; the key thing they all have in common is that they are not aimed at helping individuals, but organisations more generally.

Companies that employ enterprise developers may be general software development companies or companies that specialise in a particular sector, for example education, and produce software specifically for that sector. In some cases, it could be a large company that has its own IT services department which includes developers who produce software for that company. This could be company-specific or could be sold to other companies in the same sector.

There are also some products in this area that are aimed at small to medium-sized enterprises or companies, which provide some business support software, for example SAGE, which provides accounting software. It sells software with different capabilities and prices based on the size of company it can support.

To work in this area you would often need some knowledge (or need to gain some knowledge) of how these enterprise-level applications work, although you may be able to join a company in a junior development role and learn the business skills on the job depending on the sector.

Application programming

The line between enterprise programming and application programming can be a little blurred because enterprise programs are often considered applications themselves. This definition uses the term 'application programming' to try to differentiate development in terms of scale and use. Where enterprise software is designed to help to run a business or to support business goals, application software is designed to support the needs of individuals, which may or may not be work-related. You will doubtless see a crossover with these two types of software, for example social media, originally designed to help individuals stay in touch but now also used by some businesses particularly for things like marketing.

The range of applications is very broad and can encompass products such as games, music players, word processors, social media, fitness trackers and browsers.

This category includes apps that are designed to run on mobile phones or other mobile platforms, such as tablets or watches. These apps are often referred to as 'native apps' and are available via an app store, for example, iOS App Store or Google Play.

A very wide variety of companies provide application software; they can be huge corporates with hundreds of employees right down to one-person companies. This can encompass start-ups which will have one or two people with a great idea and that may then grow into larger companies.

Application programming: games

One specialist type of application development is games, which is almost an industry in its own right. All of the skills and knowledge mentioned in this book are still relevant for the games developer but with the addition of imagination and often artistic or graphical flair.

Games can run on many platforms from specialist games consoles to computers running a variety of hardware and operating systems. The games can be single or multi-player and may run over networks or on an individual device.

Specialist games development companies will employ this type of developer for the large gaming platforms such as games consoles, while other companies may employ games developers for educational games or games that may be embedded in a webpage.

Website development

This is where the number of modern development roles has really increased in the past few years. With the advent of the internet, companies (and individuals) have the ability to reach a much wider audience; all they need is some form of web presence. Website developers can give them that web presence, and have the capability to make web-based apps, ecommerce sites and social media sites, plus sites that can leverage mobile device hardware capabilities, for example GPS for mapping and a camera for uploading images.

The developer products described in this section have included software that could be one program, or a system comprising several programs running on a computer that provide a solution or capability. Website development is slightly different in that the product (the website) is designed to run over the internet (or intranet, a company-only network).

When you use a website you usually use a browser, for example Chrome, Edge or Firefox to get the website using a URL (the web address you type in). There could be different code running on the server-side (the computer the URL gets the website from, also known as a web host) and the client-side (that's the browser on your device). For website developers this gives rise to (at least) three possible roles: client-side (also known as front-end) developer, server-side (also known as back-end) developer and full-stack developer (does both client-side and server-side development). You may also hear about a role called UX (user experience) developer or UX engineer; they specialise in making the user interface (the front-end) of the website better for the user, for example by making the design very easy to use. UX engineers generally differ from front-end developers based on their additional training in UX design and accessibility plus the fact that they may develop components (parts) of a front-end rather than the whole front-end application.

There is no typical type of company that employs web developers; company size could be anything from one person working at home to vast corporations that employ thousands of people. Company type could be in-house developers for a specific company, an agency employing contractors, a software house or other organisation. The location options are equally diverse: developers could work remotely on a freelance basis, from home as either a full-time or part-time employee, on site at a customer's office or, more traditionally, in a company site or offices.

Embedded, real-time or firmware programming

Embedded, real-time or firmware are all specialist types of software that are used to control hardware in some way. Types of hardware could include, but are not limited to, domestic appliances, mechanical sensors, medical equipment and robots.

Software is described as being embedded when it is effectively installed on the hardware it controls; real-time and firmware are types of embedded software. Embedded software also has a wider description in that it is used to control (run) a specific machine or piece of hardware; for example, you will find embedded software in washing machines and central heating systems.

Real-time software runs within specific time limits, this is important in devices that are timing-specific. Common examples of devices that have real-time software control are heart pacemakers, anti-lock braking systems and fly-by-wire aircraft control systems.

Firmware is embedded software that is permanently stored on a hardware component. It is not generally expected that this type of software will change (hence the name 'firmware' is between hardware and software, software will change, firmware could change, hardware won't change). The firmware will run from its storage location and is very seldom updated or upgraded, if ever. An example of firmware would be the BIOS (basic input/output system) on a PC which is used in booting the system up when the PC is switched on.

Developers for this type of programming would tend to be employed by companies that develop electronic products, for example, wireless consumer products such as headphones, automatic (robotic) lawn mowers or medical devices.

THE WORLD OF SOFTWARE DEVELOPMENT

So far this chapter has introduced the overall business context for development and the types of product produced by developers. This next section looks at where development fits into a system life cycle.

Software development life cycles

A software or systems development life cycle (see Figure 2.1), as its name suggests, covers the lifetime of a product/system, from conception to eventual decommissioning. The types of task within these life cycles are generally similar across the industry; that is to say, there are nearly always these stages:

- an initial idea or requirement;
- an analysis of what is needed to produce this;
- the design for the new product;
- the production of the product;
- its deployment when it is complete;
- post-deployment support and maintenance.

You would generally use some form of methodology, management system or approach in order to manage the stages within the life cycle of a product. The difference in

Figure 2.1 Software or system life cycle

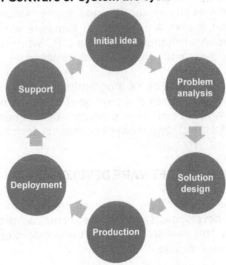

these approaches is the way the software development life cycle (SDLC) stages and tasks within the stages are arranged and carried out. While all these things may not strictly be part of coding, they are part of the context in which systems development is carried out and you may be asked to do some or parts of all of them in your role as a developer. It is therefore important to have an understanding, at least at an overview level, of what they involve.

Many different methodologies are available; the choice of which one to use may be dependent on industry sector, experience, legal requirements, the product under construction or common practice in your sector. Whichever one you use it is important to remember that there is not a one-size-fits-all methodology; selection should depend on the problem domain. A developer will need to understand the SDLC and methodology for the product or system they are working on; they should understand the stages and what their role is within those stages. As a developer you will generally work within the production stage of a SDLC; however as your career progresses you may work in other areas and as you gain experience as a developer you will probably help to influence what methodology is used to manage the stages within your product's SDLC.

Many methodologies and techniques are available to help a company or individual manage their system's life cycle. Each methodology or technique has benefits and drawbacks and should be considered in the context of the system under construction. Methodologies you might want to look into include, but are not limited to, SSADM (Structured Systems Analysis Design Method), PRINCE2 (Projects IN Controlled Environments) Agile, Kanban and Agile/Scrum.

Formal qualifications are available for some management systems and methodologies, see the following websites for more information:

- Agile/Scrum: https://www.scrum.org/
- PRINCE2 Agile: https://www.axelos.com/certifications/prince2-agile
- BCS has an extensive range of qualifications and certificates: https://www.bcs.org/get-qualified/

Waterfall and Agile

The two SDLC approaches I have chosen to cover in this book are Waterfall, an example of an older style of software development, and Agile, a modern style.

The Spiral model (Boehm, 2014), V model, Unified Process and Incremental model might also be of interest to you and are worth looking up.

Agile is described as an adaptive approach, while Waterfall is a predictive approach.

Waterfall

The first example, shown in Figure 2.2, is a very traditional life cycle model known as Waterfall. While it is no longer considered the default choice for development it is still appropriate in some cases.

Figure 2.2 Waterfall life cycle

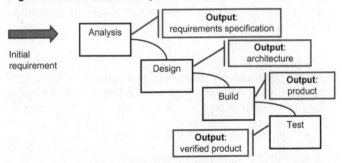

The idea behind the Waterfall life cycle is that it is a predictive approach; that is, the linear style suggests specific stages in the process, each stage having tasks and activities to complete before the next stage can start. Quite often, each stage is 'signed off' by the key stakeholders before work on the project continues.

You may also wish to add, after the Test stage, 'Install' and 'Maintain/support' to these activities (see Figure 2.3). These stages would occur after production with ongoing maintenance until the product is eventually decommissioned.

Figure 2.3 Additional, post-production stages in a Waterfall life cycle

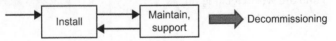

The Waterfall model illustrated in Figure 2.2 is sometimes modernised to give the design shown in Figure 2.4. This shows a cyclical life cycle where each phase can feed back into a previous stage for improvements and ongoing increments.

Figure 2.4 Modernised Waterfall life cycle

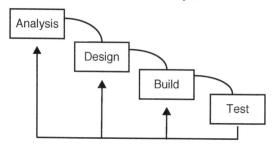

In order to understand the types of activity covered in each of the stages in the Waterfall life cycle I have provided a brief list below. Note that this is not a complete list, just a summary of the main activities typically carried out.

- Analysis
  - Investigating the problem domain, learning about the product that is needed to solve a given problem or requirement.
  - Possibly also investigating other potential solutions and considering why the solution proposed is the best choice.
  - Defining the scope for the product, what it may and may not do (its features and boundaries). This analysis provides the requirements for the product which can produce a requirements specification.
- Design
  - This can include the design for the whole system as well as for distinct parts of the system including the

data, functionality, screen layouts, reports, security and architecture.

- The design might be expressed using diagrams, text documents, models or prototypes (simple mock-ups of part of the proposed product, which might go on to be part of the product itself).

- Build – the main area of focus for the developer

  - The production of the code for the product. A developer may write anything from a complete system, to small parts of that system.

  - May be done individually or as part of a team.

  - May include creating screen layouts and report design.

  - Includes debugging and some testing.

  - Usually involves some form of documentation.

  - The language used to write the code depends on the domain, the platform that the product is intended for and the company employing the developer.

- Test

  - Various levels and types of testing are expected within software production.

  - A developer is usually expected to test the components they have built.

  - Other testing levels may be required depending on the developers' organisation or sector.

- Install (deployment)

  - This is the installation of the software to its desired platform. This may be done via a tool to bundle the product and make an installation file which may be deployed by a USB drive or similar media, or, more commonly, via a network, for example, by download from the internet.

- Maintain or support
  - This could involve fixing errors found after the product has been deployed, or it could involve enhancements or improvements to the product that can be added incrementally after deployment.
  - Other aspects of support may be compatibility-related, ensuring the product works on the latest operating system for its platform and fixing and issuing updates as necessary.

The benefits of a Waterfall approach are as follows:

- There are structured stages, in a specific order.
- The Waterfall model is familiar to many, it has been around for a long time.
- The Waterfall model is sequential, one stage is completed before moving to the next, and there are often gatekeepers at each stage.
- Documentation is produced at every stage of the product's development.
- Developers and customers agree on what will be delivered early in the life cycle which should make planning, monitoring and design easier.
- Progress should be more easily measured, as the scope of the work is known in advance.

Disadvantages of a Waterfall approach include the following:

- Requirements should be fixed and complete before production begins; this could involve a lot of time spent up front before any lines of code are written. This could be problematic for systems that have a specific delivery date, time limit or fixed price contract.
- Rigidity of requirements and therefore of the product being built. Because the requirements are gathered 'up front' any changes needed may be difficult to add later.

- Changes to requirements may cause confusion, wasted effort or a project restart.

- The working software can only be seen at the end of the process. This means that if there is a change in business practices or a fundamental change needed in the way the product works it may not be spotted until right at the end.

- The product is unknown to the customer until it is delivered at the end. This means that feedback from the customer is not received until the product has been built, meaning that changes will be more expensive to add.

- There can be a lack of visibility – teams don't realise they are behind schedule until later in the life cycle.

- The amount of time given to the later stages (e.g. testing) is often squeezed by overrunning timescales in earlier stages.

- Emphasis on getting information right up front, which puts pressure on people to decide early and to remember 'everything' they want in the new product in the beginning.

Waterfall life cycles are best suited for:

- Projects that require fixed stages and deadlines, accountability or legal auditing.

- Short, simple projects where theoretically, little can go wrong.

- Projects with changing project teams that depend on extensive documentation.

- Projects with stable, known requirements, for example, projects that may have been done before, where chances of surprises or changes during the development process are relatively low.

- Projects where change is complex and expensive: this could be because a change may result in a large amount of wasted time, work or money or because a change of direction would not be possible, for example if the hardware had already been bought and installed. This is distinct from Agile projects which are designed to deal with changing requirements. If change is complex or expensive the project will not allow deviations from the original plan, requirements or design.

Agile

In February 2001, at a meeting of software developers, several of those developers got together and discussed their different approaches to development with a view to trying to come up with an approach that worked well for both creators and consumers of a product. The outcome of this meeting was the **Manifesto for Agile Software Development** (Beck et al., 2001). Several participants from that meeting went on to found the Agile Alliance (2001).

The Agile Alliance website describes Agile as:

an umbrella term for a set of frameworks and practices based on the values and principles expressed in the Manifesto for Agile Software Development and the 12 Principles behind it.

This is a summary of those 12 principles from the Agile Manifesto (see the original list in Beck et al., 2001):

- Early and continuous delivery of valuable software.
- Welcoming changing requirements, even late in development.
- Delivering working software frequently, from a couple of weeks to a couple of months, with a preference to the shorter timescale.
- Business people and developers working together daily throughout the project.
- Building projects around motivated individuals. Giving them the environment and support they need, and trusting them to get the job done.
- Conducting face-to-face conversation as the most efficient and effective method of communication.

- Using working software as the primary measure of progress.

- Sponsors, developers and users maintaining a constant pace indefinitely.

- Continuously paying attention to technical excellence and good design, which enhances agility.

- Working with simplicity in mind – the art of maximising the amount of work not done.

- Utilising self-organising teams, from where the best architectures, requirements and designs emerge.

- The team reflecting, at regular intervals, on how to become more effective, then tuning and adjusting its behaviour accordingly.

Agile practices promote adaptive planning, evolutionary development, early delivery and continuous improvement of both the product under construction and the process being used to construct the product. It also encourages:

- Rapid and flexible response to change. In a dynamically changing business world, being able to change direction or deliver products before your competitors may be the difference between survival and closure.

- Timely and regular delivery of business value through short sprints (these are the time-boxes in which development takes place).

- Feedback from stakeholders and the team developing the system.

- Collaboration among stakeholders and system development team.

- Prioritised functionality, meaning the features that are most important are delivered first. This can be particularly helpful if the product is part of a trial or a prototype.

Agile does not tell you how to implement the ideas listed in the manifesto. People who use Agile use a set of common practices and often use a methodology too. Among the most commonly used methodologies are:

- Adaptive software development (ASD), created by Jim Highsmith.
- Agile modelling, created by Scott Ambler.
- Dynamic systems development method (DSDM), created by the DSDM Consortium.
- Extreme programming (XP), created by Kent Beck, Ward Cunningham and Ron Jeffries.
- Feature-driven development (FDD), created by Jeff De Luca.
- Kanban (development), created by David J. Anderson.
- Lean software development, created by Mary and Tom Poppendieck.
- Scrum, created by Jeff Sutherland, Mike Beedle and Ken Schwaber.

Of these, probably the most widely used is **Scrum**.

Scrum
Scrum is a product development methodology used to produce complex products (it is not just used for software). It has a 'to do' list (the product backlog) and it completes items from the list, in priority order, in short time-boxes (sprints). Each item in the sprint is done to completion. This could encompass design, building, testing, documenting, deploying or whatever is deemed necessary to complete that item.

It has **Roles** (what you do) + **Events**/**Ceremonies** (when you do it) + **Artefacts** (what you produce).

The roles are:

Product owner – all about the product: the what and why. The product owner will identify stakeholders and create an overview of the product, what it is and who it is aimed at. They will also create and manage the product backlog so that the product is built in the best way possible.

Development team member – all about the build; everything that is needed in order to complete the work selected for the sprint. The mix of people inside the development team can change from one sprint to another but does not change during a sprint. The team is multi-disciplined and self-organising.

Scrum Master – all about the process (a Scrum expert and champion). This person is the enabler for the team; they ensure the Scrum process is understood and enacted and they help to sort out problems that may be hindering progress.

The events/ceremonies are:

The **Sprint** – this is a container for all other events in Scrum including (but not only) production; it lasts up to one month. It lets the Scrum team break the development work down into tasks ensuring the most important items are completed early on.

Sprint planning – a meeting where the Scrum team decide what is to be done in the sprint, including estimates and planning. Various techniques are used for estimation, such as Planning Poker or Affinity Estimation.

Planning Poker and Affinity Estimation are two of the most popular estimation techniques. They help developers estimate effort in 'story points', which indicate how difficult something is to build compared with other items they are building for the product. An example could be when building a website, a search feature would be more difficult to build than a paragraph of text which includes a picture, and therefore the search feature would have an estimate with a higher number of 'story points' than the paragraph of text with the image.

Both techniques use number values (in the form of either paper or electronic 'playing' cards) to estimate a features value. The difference between the two styles is that Planning Poker gives a value to each feature, one at a time, whereas Affinity Estimation groups the features into 'like difficulty' first then decides on a value that will be applied to each of the features. (Affinity Estimation is a better technique to use if the team is new to Agile development or unfamiliar with Agile estimation techniques.)

Daily Scrum (also known as a daily stand-up) – a 15-minute meeting where each member of the development team states what they have done in the previous day, what they will be doing on that day and any blockers (problems) they have that may hinder progress.

Sprint review – a consideration (and possible demonstration) of the work completed during the sprint where the Scrum team can get feedback from any stakeholders that may be present. They can discuss what went well, what didn't go well and revise the product backlog.

Sprint retrospective – a consideration of how the Scrum process itself worked, where attendees consider possible improvements for the next sprint and create a plan for improvements. The Scrum Master may introduce and demonstrate new tools that have been identified for use in the next sprint in order to help the development team.

The artefacts are:

Product backlog – the to-do list, this is an ordered or prioritised list of product requirements, features, functions, dependency needs, enhancements (change requests) and bug fixes.

Sprint backlog – the to-do list for the time-box, the product backlog items selected for the sprint, plus the plan for delivery.

If multiple teams are working on the same product there is a shared product backlog but each team will have its own sprint backlog.

Progress monitoring – Scrum prescribes that you should keep track of progress so that you know where the project is at any given time. This is often done via burn down charts (a diagramming method used to chart effort or time remaining; when done well they show at a glance whether you are on target to achieve your projected product development).

For full details on the Scrum methodology see the Scrum guide: https://www.scrum.org/resources/scrum-guide

To see the whole Scrum process summarised (by Neon Rain, 2019) see Figure 2.5.

Agile advantages and disadvantages
Advantages for the business of using an Agile approach are:

- Faster delivery of business benefit, by phased delivery or demonstrably working product early in the life cycle.

- Higher quality deliverables as each deliverable is completed (this could mean designed, built, tested and documented or whatever the team deems is 'complete' for the purpose of that project).

- Reduced risk – early detection of failing projects (due to earlier feedback). With work being done in small increments, if something is wrong you have only lost a small amount of time, relatively speaking.

- Increased flexibility, being able to adapt to changing business needs or requirements.

Figure 2.5 Agile Scrum framework at a glance (Source: Reproduced (with no changes made) by kind permission of Neon Rain (2019). Licence: https://creativecommons.org/licenses/by-nd/3.0/nz/)

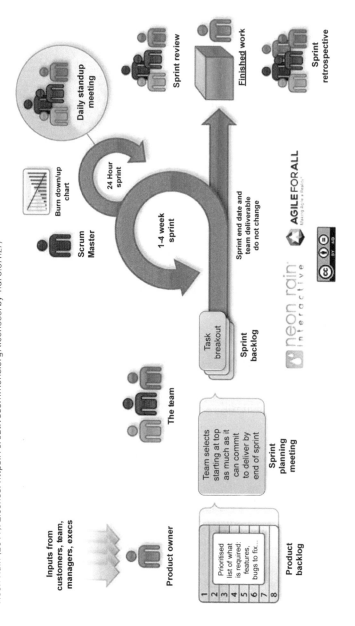

- Greater project visibility. I find this methodology helps people understand the development process better, as they are more involved in it.

- Improved teamwork and cooperation (which may lead to improved morale).

- Continuous improvement of the product.

- Iterative planning, as time is not spent up front gathering every detail about everything (some of which may not be implemented in the new system).

- Improved communication and collaboration.

The benefits for a developer of using an Agile approach are as follows:

- Clear expectations set and communicated frequently for each sprint.

- Success is clearly defined and a clear definition of complete is provided (known as the definition of 'Done').

- Issues are raised early on (and escalated or dealt with by the Scrum Master).

- New skills for the team, broader skill base.

- Team support.

- Collaboration within the team and with the stakeholders.

- Project visibility, as one of the requirements of working in an Agile way is to make all the information relating to the build visible. One example of this are 'Scrum boards' (see Figure 2.6).

Possible disadvantages of using an Agile approach include the following:

- It takes practice to do it well: some companies or teams give up too soon.

- It can seem chaotic to people outside the Agile/Scrum process.

Figure 2.6 An example Scrum board

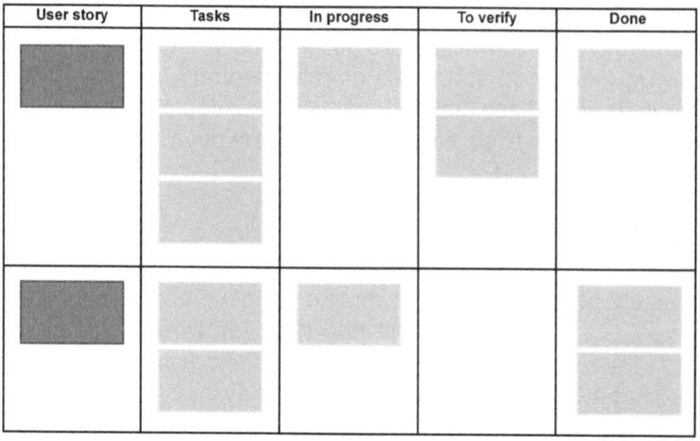

User story	Tasks	In progress	To verify	Done

- It relies on close collaboration with the customer.
- It is not suitable for all products. Agile is a favoured style for projects which meet the following criteria:
  - poorly defined or incomplete requirements;
  - shorter timescales;
  - the customer wants to use iterative features during the build process (features that are added a bit at a time as the product evolves);
  - the development team is not too large;
  - customer involvement is possible.
- While you still create documentation in Agile projects it is typically not as comprehensive as that created in projects managed with more traditional techniques. This might be a problem for companies that need extensive audit trails or specifications for legal reasons.

Beyond programming: deployment, maintenance and support

Some developers will spend a percentage of their time involved in bug fixing and amending or maintaining older (known as legacy) code. These tasks, along with post-deployment support, are considered to be a normal part of the developer role.

SUMMARY

This chapter looked at the context for development including where development is used, and where and when development fits into a software or systems life cycle. It also began to look at what developers do in the context of systems development. The next chapter will look at the role in more detail, including what skills are necessary to fulfil the role plus the types of responsibility you should expect to have as a software developer.

3 THE ROLE OF SOFTWARE DEVELOPER

> Prolific developers don't always write a lot of code, instead they solve a lot of problems. The two things are not the same.
>
> J. Chambers, Creator of the S programming language

This chapter looks at the role of developer in more detail, specifically what the skills and knowledge needed for the role are, and what responsibilities you will have as a software developer.

Three key technical skills allow you to focus on coding. These skills are:

- logical or analytical thinking;
- knowledge of a programming language;
- an understanding of data.

There are also some key 'soft skills' that are necessary for working in modern development environments. These are:

- communication;
- teamwork.

As a software developer you will have a number of responsibilities. These responsibilities are likely to include:

- understanding requirements;
- cross-platform development;
- understanding and ensuring quality;
- testing and debugging;
- maintenance and refactoring;

- preparing documentation;
- consideration of non-functional requirements;
- keeping security in mind.

WHAT TYPES OF INDUSTRY OR SECTOR DO DEVELOPERS WORK IN?

Most people think of developers as working in the computer industry; in reality, so many areas of our lives are touched by software. Anything electronic would usually have a control program, from washing machines to aeroplanes, cars to smart phones and all manner of devices in between.

Many sectors and business areas need software, so almost any sphere of interest for you may provide opportunities for developer roles. Some areas will need very specialist knowledge: for example, those developers engaged in scientific software development. For others, knowledge can be developed on the job, for example, in software development for banking. There are also technologies that are evolving and emergent such as AI (artificial intelligence), Blockchain, machine learning, 3D printing, augmented reality, robotics including nanobots (tiny little robots that work inside the human body), and internet of things (IoT). All of these new technologies will provide new opportunities for developers. While some technologies, for example nanobots, have specific sectors (science/medical), others, for example augmented reality, have cross-sector scope and appeal.

Even areas that may not need software developers directly, for example florists, may still use software to run the business, to analyse data, to place orders, to get design ideas and to sell their products online. Opportunities exist in the public, private and voluntary sectors encompassing areas such as government, education, energy, transport, manufacturing, conservation, finance, science, design, agriculture, telecoms and communications, services, entertainment and utilities, to name but a few. So, as a developer you could find yourself working in a company known for diamond mining, banking or entertainment, beyond just the possibility of working for a technology company.

WHAT DO DEVELOPERS DO TO CREATE PRODUCTS?

In the simplest sense, a developer uses a programming language to write a set of instructions which cause an electronic device to carry out a task or tasks: for example to display a webpage or colourise a picture.

In reality, a developer has a variety of skills and responsibilities that help them understand a broad range of associated concepts, technologies, industries, tools and environments in order to develop the product they are creating. The developer will need to understand the 'problem' they are trying to solve; they may need to design the product, write it, document it and test it. While this book introduces a wide range of skills and responsibilities you may have as a developer, the ones you need for a specific job can vary greatly. A person writing software to control a nuclear reactor will probably need some different skills and knowledge from those of a person who develops webpages.

SKILLS

In this section we will consider the key skills a software developer will need.

Let's look at the basic set of skills first. In order to write the instructions that make up a program (the coding part of a developer's job) you will need the three key skills mentioned at the start of this chapter: logical or analytical thinking (to understand the problem, for planning and design); knowledge of a programming language (to write the instructions); and an understanding of data (which will be used in the program).

Abraham Lincoln once said 'Give me six hours to chop down a tree and I will spend the first four sharpening the axe.'

Translated into software development terms, this means that you don't just dive straight into coding; you spend some time in the understanding and planning phase.

Logical thinking

The first skill we will consider is thinking: logical or analytical thinking to be precise. Consider the nature of code and the nature of computers or other devices that we create products for. They can only do what they are told (AI aside, but that's another discussion altogether) so a developer needs to be very precise about what instructions they write and how they write those instructions. Coding needs knowledge of both a programming language (the syntax), plus logic, problem solving and creativity (how to use the language to create a program).

Sometimes on the courses I teach, one of the practical exercises I give to new developers is the cheese challenge. You could try this if you have the time or resources (it's good fun done in teams or groups with other new developers).

- Describe how to make cheese sandwiches ... your intended audience are aliens or robots with no previous experience of sandwich making.
  - get a pen and paper, write down the steps;
  - be precise and detailed;
  - maximum time for this task is 15 minutes.

- Swap your instructions with another person or team, if you are working in groups or teams.

- Read the instructions and consider the following questions:

  - Is there a list of requirements up front, e.g. bread, cheese, knife, plus what quantities and what types are needed?

  - Are any parts of the procedure missing, e.g. opening the butter tub?

  - Have any assumptions been made, e.g. the bread is ready sliced?

  - Would the sandwich that is made using these instructions meet with your approval, e.g. thickness of butter layer or cheese?

  - How do you judge if your sandwich is 'ready' or 'good'?

Sometimes I get a volunteer to make a cheese sandwich based on the instructions. You would be amazed at how easy it is to miss out simple parts of the process (and how funny it can be watching someone try to follow the instructions exactly).

So how is this logical thinking or coding? Programming is a list of instructions that tell a computer how to complete a task; it is like a recipe that comprises ingredients, instructions and tasting as you go along. You need to be able to work out how to create this recipe and, like a recipe, there are many right ways to get what you want (and quite a few wrong ways too).

Here's how the simile translates to the software development domain:

- User requirements: You need to ask the user important questions about what they want such as:

- How many sandwiches do they want?
- When do they want them?
- Do they want them hot or cold?

- Ingredients = variables and components (things that you declare up front that you will use later in your program, for example, to store data in).

- Instructions = the code may contain instructions such as:

  - A sequence – steps that always happen, no variations.

  - Loops – repetition; in a recipe this could be where you add seasoning and then taste it (repeat as necessary).

  - If statements – choices that control what you do; in a recipe for example, if you like pickle add it in, if you don't, then don't use it.

  - Components (parts of a program; these can be 'ready-made' or built by the developer) – in a recipe, for example, using a shop-bought sliced loaf of bread (you are not going to bake your own bread during the sandwich-making process; it would take you far too long to make the sandwich). In development a similar principle is using external code libraries written by someone else, or previously created by you at some stage prior to being needed in your current project.

- Tasting = testing:

  - Does what you created meet the user's requirements – did you make a thick sandwich, a toasted sandwich, a stack of sandwiches?

Considering all those things, you might want to rewrite your sandwich making instructions. Think of the following if you do:

- Have you defined your requirements up front?
- How many of the items you require are 'ready-made', e.g. the bread?
- Have you built in tasting, or tests (called inspection points, in programming)?
- What questions would you ask your end user to determine success?
- Could you make suggestions to improve the process or the finished product?

Extending the cheese sandwich idea further, you can ensure the sandwich is safe to eat by making sure all the ingredients are within their use by date. This equates to **security** in development terms and making sure your end users are safe, which can also relate to **legal requirements**.

You can make your life easier by getting everything together before you start making the sandwich and by keeping your workspace clean and tidy so you can find things when you need them. In development this would be **analysis** and **design**, understanding what you are making and planning what you need, being thorough and organised. It also equates to **good practice**.

You can ensure a **quality** product and customer satisfaction by asking the relevant questions of your **end user**; **communication** is vital and the same applies in development.

After you have delivered (**deployed**) the sandwich, you may need to do some follow-up or **support** work on the sandwich, offering pickle as an enhancement perhaps; in development terms that's incremental development.

Finally, you could clear away the empty plates after the sandwich has been consumed, that's following through the entire sandwich **life cycle**. Of course, you could just buy a sandwich, that's **outsourcing** or buying off the shelf software.

The developer needs to be able to use **analytical thinking** to ask relevant questions, work out what the problem is and how to solve it. **Logic** and **problem-solving** skills will help you to plan the steps that need to be taken for your project and what resources you need. Generally, you need to break a problem down into smaller task-based parts, and when you write the code you write it in small 'chunks', variously known as subroutines, functions or procedures. The smaller the 'chunks' of code, the easier it usually is to test and maintain that code. **Creativity** will help with building the program: designing new ways to solve the problem. Good **standards** and **good practices** will help you to create good quality code that is reusable, easy to read and easy to maintain.

Knowledge of a programming language

The programming language you use is very dependent on what you are creating and the company or sector you work in. You can start off with one language (I started with Cobol) and end up using a very different language (I now do a lot of work in JavaScript). What you learn and when can depend on your changing role, your company's needs, emerging platforms and technologies, and current development trends.

If you undertake formal education or qualifications, for example at university, the language you learn may be imposed upon you (many universities teach Java for example). Alternatively, you may choose to learn a language in order to create a particular product, change career direction or in response to a request from your employer. Whatever language you start with, it is common in the industry to learn different languages and continue to learn new development skills.

You will be expected to keep up with new versions or capabilities of your current language. Some languages and libraries change frequently, with new capabilities being available often (maybe several times a year); others are more static, with updates less frequently. Languages relating to web development are particularly prone to updates of versions, enhancements of capabilities or new responses to emergent technologies or needs.

Keeping up to date with a language refers not only to the syntax but also to its use. There may be new best practices for you to follow, more efficient ways to use the language, or additional capabilities (things that you could not previously do with the language but now you can). The software that you write will also give you opportunities for learning; each new product has the capacity to be different from the one before. As well as the language, you will also have to understand the environment that language needs and the platform that it runs on. It may have dependencies on tools and specific systems or methodologies in order to work.

> Programming, and therefore programming languages, have been around for more than 70 years. Over that time the number of languages has blossomed, with many falling in and out of favour. Early programming done in binary, machine code or Assembly Language is uncommon now and each year the top 20 most used languages has some winners and losers.

What is the best language to learn? That is a difficult question to answer because, as mentioned earlier, there are many dependencies. Let's take a brief look at language popularity and use.

The website Stack Overflow is well known in the development sector. It provides help with questions via a community of developers (https://stackoverflow.com/). Stack Overflow has been carrying out surveys for a few years to find out what languages its users use for development. In 2019 there were nearly 90,000 respondents.[1] Their findings showed the following languages (in order of popularity):

- JavaScript;
- HTML/CSS;
- SQL;
- Python;
- Java;
- Bash/Shell/PowerShell;
- C#;
- PHP;
- TypeScript;
- C++;
- C;
- Ruby.

Before rushing out to learn any of these languages, a few points to consider. First, the nature of the respondents. Looking at the survey results, based on the job titles submitted it is likely they do a lot of web-based development; therefore the most popular languages reflect that platform. Second, the languages listed are not all 'software development' languages; while HTML, CSS and SQL are types of language, they have very specific applications within the types of software we are discussing in this book. HTML is a mark-up language used to define the content of a webpage, CSS is used to style the contents of a webpage, and SQL is a query language used to manipulate, query and organise data. Bash/Shell is also very specialised: it is a command processing language widely used to carry out actions on a Unix-based system. While the languages themselves are all valuable to the developer you could not develop a full product using 'just' CSS; you would need to combine CSS with HTML and JavaScript for example.

Before thinking about the programming language (or more likely languages) you want to learn, you should consider the type of product you would like to work on and the sort of industry or sector you would be interested in working in. For example, firmware is often written in C or C++; apps for mobile phones may be written in Objective-C or Java; games may be written in C, C++ or Java; commercial software can use a variety of languages, C# is very popular. That said, all of the above products could be written in other languages; some games are written in HTML, CSS and JavaScript for example, because while there are commonly used languages, there are also exceptions and no hard and fast rules.

The really important thing with whatever language you learn is to understand the logic of it; logical thinking is a transferable skill across all development languages. Practise problem solving and learn the good practices for the sector and languages you work in.

There's more on programming languages in the next chapter.

Understanding and using data

THE DIFFERENCE BETWEEN DATA AND INFORMATION

The date '13 March 1975' is a piece of data; put that data in context, for example as a birthday, and it becomes information. So, information tells you something, it is data in context.

As a developer you will need to understand what the data that is needed by your program will be, how it will be stored and formatted, its context and what you will need to do in your program to use that data. You may need to organise the data yourself or consume data that is already in a given format. That data could then be used as input to some part of your program in order to inform or control actions or processes (Figure 3.1). Alternatively, the data could be output as some form of information (Figure 3.2), whether that is output to a screen or a report depends on the application. Finally, in some cases, the data may be input and output with your program being used to transform the data in some way (Figure 3.3).

As well as using stored data you may get data input from a user, for example when a user places an order and adds products to a shopping basket.

Figure 3.1 An example of data used as input to control actions or processes

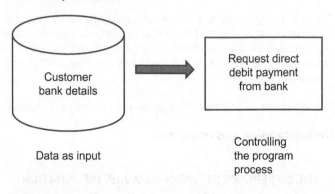

Customer bank details

Request direct debit payment from bank

Data as input

Controlling the program process

Figure 3.2 An example of data used as output in some form of information

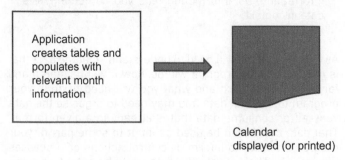

Application creates tables and populates with relevant month information

Calendar displayed (or printed)

Figure 3.3 An example of data used for input and output with data transformation

Data as input   Data transformation   Information output

Within development there are many types of **data storage**, these could include:

- Flat file – a text- or binary-based file which may be comma separated or may use another (possibly proprietary) format.

- Hierarchical – sometimes known as a tree or node structure. Nodes are referred to as 'parents' and 'children'; each 'child' in the structure has a single 'parent' (a parent node can have zero to many children but a child can only have one parent).

- Network – also a type of parent–child structure but each item can have an unlimited number of parents or children (known as owners or members).

- Relational – record-based, with links (relationships) formed between records.

The **physical location** of the data could vary, they could be stored locally on the same machine as the data user or across a network, either centralised (all data in one location on your network), distributed (data spread across various locations on your network) or cloud-based (data spread across various locations on external servers or networks).

There are also different **formats** of data that can be exchanged between systems: for example, when a data feed is sent from a social media site to a webpage that data may need to be organised in a specific way. Some of the most widely used formats include:

- JSON (JavaScript Object Notation);
- XML (eXtensible Markup Language);
- EDI (Electronic Data Interchange).

You could use one or more of these data formats in your program. Each application could have a completely different set of data requirements.

This section will go into a little more detail about two of the most commonly used types of data; that is, one data format type (JSON) and one data storage type (relational databases) along with other useful information related to using data in development.

DATA TYPES

A data type is simply a definition of the sort of data that is expected; for example, a name could be a string (text-based) data type, a customer number could be an integer (a whole number, no decimal places), a salary could be a real number (one with decimal places). The exact data types available during development will vary with the data storage type or format or programming language you are using.

JSON

JSON is a simple data-interchange format; it is based on the object structure from the JavaScript Programming Language. Originally specified by Douglas Crockford (n.d.), JSON is a collection of **name/value** (also known as **property:value**) pairs. Because it uses JavaScript's simple object notation structure it is easy to use in JavaScript although it can also be used in programs written in other languages.

This short example of JSON formatted data shows the sort of information you might use for customer contact data:

```
{
"title": "Ms",
"fullName": "Jane Doe",
"email": "jd@here.com",
"mobile": "01234567890",
"lastContact": "Thu, 23 Dec 2010 14:21:21
GMT"
}
```

The example shown describes the contact data for one customer: it shows five property:value pairs, the property names are 'title', 'fullName', 'email', 'mobile' and 'lastContact' and each property has a corresponding value.

Many websites online allow you to access their data via JSON, for example Flickr, Twitter and Facebook. The sites that allow you to access their data will often have documentation that gives examples of how to get the data and how to use it in various programming languages. The UK government also makes data publicly available in a variety of formats, see https://data.gov.uk/

If you want to see a real-life example, this URL will give you Flickr data in a JSON format.

https://api.flickr.com/services/feeds/photos_public.gne?nojs oncallback=1&format=json&tags=trees

Relational databases

In development one of the commonest forms of data storage to work with is some form of relational database. The particular database, the way the data is stored on the disk and where the data is stored (locally or across a network) is specific to each database and system. Many different database products are available, for example MySQL, SQL Server, Oracle, Azure SQL Database.

DATABASE TERMINOLOGY

Database – A database is a collection of logically related data that can be defined and controlled independently of user applications. They are made up of tables (for example 'Customers' or 'Accounts') which consist of rows (typically one row for each customer or account) which are, in turn, made up of columns (each of which is a piece of data related to the row). You may hear alternative terminology that uses the word 'record' instead of 'row' and 'field' instead of 'column'.

Database management system – A database management system (DBMS) is the software used for developing and managing a database independently of any programs that use the data.

Entity – something which an organisation collects and stores data on, for example a customer, an order or a bank account.

Attribute – a data element associated with an entity, for example a customer number, customer name, customer address or current balance.

Relationship – the term used for the association between entities, for example a customer is related to an order by the relationship 'places', in that a customer places an order.

Identifier – an entity has an identifier; that is, an attribute that uniquely identifies an occurrence of a particular entity among many occurrences of the same entity, e.g. the identifier for a customer might be Customer Number. An identifier is sometimes called a Primary Key.

Whether you consume, or design and consume the data that is required for your program you will need to understand that data and its relationships, format and use. There are many different ways of documenting and explaining data. Companies will generally use a variety of styles depending on their chosen database, company standards and project management methodology.

Data is usually described by some form of entity relationship model (ERM) which is made up of two parts. These are:

- Entity relationship description – a written description of all the entities, their attributes and relationships.
- Entity relationship diagram (ERD) – a pictorial representation of the entities and their relationships.

Table 3.1 shows an example entity relationship description that could make up part of the entity, attribute and relationship documentation for a customer and order relationship.

In the written descriptions you have entries for every entity, attribute and relationship in your database; this means entity relationship modelling can stretch to many pages of information. In Table 3.1 I have just shown one example of each type of description (one entity – the customer, one attribute – the customer identifier and one relationship – that between the customer and order).

Note that in the text descriptions a 'Constraint' is a limitation or special circumstance that exists for the item being described. The 'Requirement' is a reference back to the document (the requirements) that requested this particular bit of functionality or data.

As well as text descriptions you will also have diagrams to show entities and relationships. Figure 3.4 shows an ERD which models two entities and their relationship, the two entities in this case are customer and order. You can see the entities in the boxes, a line that shows there is a relationship and the text which describes the relationship.

Table 3.1 An example of entity relationship descriptions

Entity description	
Identifier:	E1
Name:	Customer
Description:	Any person who has requested a catalogue
Attributes:	Customer identifier (string) **Primary Key**
	Customer name (string) **Mandatory**
	Customer address (string) **Mandatory**
	Postcode (string) **Mandatory**
	Latest catalogue (y/n)
Constraints:	Customer removed after two years without any orders
Assumptions:	None
Comments:	The date the customer joined will be required
Requirement:	RQ1-5, 8 and 12

Attribute description	
Identifier:	A32
Name:	Customer identifier
Description:	The unique identifier of a customer. Composed of region code and customer number
Data type:	String
Data values:	Region code (N, S, E, W, SC, WE, IR) Customer number (8 digits [0 to 9])
Constraints:	Customer number is only unique within each region.

(Continued)

Table 3.1 (Continued)

Comments:	There is currently no separate use of, or requirement for, region code in any system functionality but it may need to be broken out if sales data is required by region.
Owner:	Sales
Requirement:	RQ1, 8 and 12

Relationship description

Identifier:	R1
Name:	Orders
Entities linked:	Customer and order
Description:	The linking of customers and their orders. This relationship is used in both directions.
Definition:	A customer **may** place **0**, **1** or **many** orders
	An order **must** be placed by **1** customer
Assumptions:	Joint orders are not made
Comments:	None
Requirement:	RQ1-5, 8 and 12

Figure 3.4 Simple ERD showing customer and order

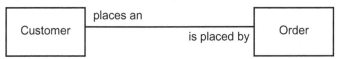

In ERD it is normal to show the relationship between the entities by the number of potential entries in that relationship (referred to as its degree or cardinality). For example, a customer may place many orders but an order can only be placed by one customer. This is a one to many relationship, it is written as 1:M (note that we could have a customer on our database who has not placed any orders yet, they could have just requested a catalogue but have not ordered yet, so technically the customer order relationship is zero to many 0:M). Figure 3.5 shows this using ERD. It reads as 'a customer places zero to many orders, an order is placed by one and only one customer'. The two vertical lines next to the customer box means one and only one, the symbol next to the order box (the circle and a symbol known as a crows foot) means zero to many.

Figure 3.5 Simple ERD showing customer and order with relationship symbols

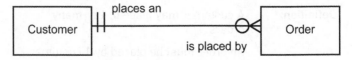

Other examples of relationships in data could be:

- Zero to one – for example a bank customer may or may not have an ISA account.

- Zero or one to many – for example a training course could have no students signed up or it could have one to many.

- One to one – for example a pension can belong to one and only one employee.

An entity has one or more attributes (the data that is stored about an entity); an ERD will show the entities required in a database plus their relationships, while the **attributes** will show the data items relating to those entities. When a database is designed the identifier (primary key) is named for each entity.

It is then necessary to document the remaining attributes for an entity either via entity relationship descriptions shown in Table 3.1 or via a simple diagram. Figure 3.6 shows a very simple example of some of the attributes that may belong to the customer entity.

Figure 3.6 Simple entity attribute diagram

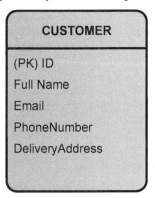

Multiple attributes can be 'grouped' under a Group Name, for example, Full Name (first name, middle name, last name).

There are entire books written on the subject of diagramming and describing data and systems so this book will not go any further on data documentation techniques.

SQL

In order to use data, you need to access the relevant parts of the database in your code. To do this you normally use SQL (usually pronounced seeqwal) which is a language used with relational databases. An example of a SQL statement used to get all the information on a particular customer row or record might look like this:

```
SELECT * FROM customer WHERE CustomerID = 123456
```

That reads as 'get all the attributes (fields/columns) from the customer record (row) for the customer with the ID 123456'.

Normalisation
While all developers need to understand how data is structured, not every developer will be expected to design databases. If you need to design the data you will use – that is, work out what the entities, attributes, relationships and so on are, and design or build the database structure – you will need some database-specific training. During the training you should learn about normalisation, which is a set of rules and guidelines that help you create well-designed databases.

Communication

Modern development practices emphasise communication as a necessary skill in the development process. It is needed in order to understand software requirements, ask relevant questions and present possible solutions.

While you do not need to be an accomplished public speaker, you do need to be comfortable chatting to people of all skill and responsibility levels. Agile methodologies in particular emphasise face-to-face communication and collaboration with both your team and your end users or other stakeholders.

It is also useful to note that as well as being able to talk to people about your work you also need to understand when that would not be appropriate. Some systems and software may need to be discussed only within the team or group that employs you. Consider work covered by the Official Secrets Act or products that need to have high security because of the General Data Protection Regulation (GDPR) or legal restrictions, for example banking or credit card payments. You need to understand security and safety in the products that you produce and in your working environment.

Don't be put off if you think you don't meet all of these criteria; you can work on it and there will still be a role for you in development.

Teamwork

There are no hard and fast rules that govern how much of a product you will create as a developer. You may start off with the simplest amount of code which could be, for instance, a small subroutine, refactoring existing code, creating a banner animation for a website or working on a partially complete piece of code, or you could be required to develop an entire product or system. Irrespective of how much of the product you create you will not be creating it alone; even if you write all the code you will still be working with other people who may have various roles in the production process; this is why teamwork is vital for the modern development role.

There are also no hard and fast rules as to how big a team you will work in. Modern methodologies such as Agile/Scrum emphasise teamwork; the Scrum team is expected to be a self-organising, supportive, multi-disciplined group of between three and nine developers for instance. Modern techniques also encourage pair programming and the use of collaborative tools such as Jira.

When you are working with other people in meetings or communicating in other ways, for example by email, always ensure you understand the key points under discussion and crucially who is responsible for carrying out any action points that stem from any meetings or discussions you may have.

Another handy tip for meetings with your team is to ensure you understand what the meeting is about (and if a decision is expected out of the meeting). It sounds like an obvious thing to say but it is all too common to turn up for a meeting unprepared and be expected to make a statement or decision on some topic. Find out what the meeting is for and what is expected of you so that you are not caught out.

The FutureLearn site has some excellent free short courses on communication skills and teamwork, see https://www.futurelearn.com/courses/categories/business-and-management-courses/communication-skills

SOFTWARE DEVELOPER RESPONSIBILITIES

The first part of this chapter looked at the skills or knowledge you needed in order to do the main part of a developer's role; that is, the coding (you need logical or analytical thinking, knowledge of a programming language and an understanding of data). However coding does not cover everything you need to work as a developer; there are also other associated responsibilities which will be covered in the next few pages. These are key things you need to be able to do to make you a 'good' developer, which is to develop the right products well with a view to quality and maintainability.

Understanding requirements

Broadly speaking, the traditional requirements phase of a life cycle allows you to obtain and document the requirements for a new system. The process traditionally has multiple stages; how much detail is gathered before the coding starts and how that detail is documented is dependent on methodology, business context and product.

It is not generally part of the role of a developer to perform requirements engineering, certainly not in a junior role, but you will need to understand the requirements that you are given as they form part of the product specification. There may be a variety of diagramming and documentation types used; you will need to understand them and be able to ask **meaningful questions** based on the information you are given.

This book will introduce two popular techniques for documenting requirements, use cases (which come from Unified Modelling Language (UML)) and User Stories (a popular technique in Agile).

UML and use cases

UML is used by developers to better understand the problem domain. UML is actually a set of different modelling techniques which are grouped together under one title. A model abstracts the essential details of the underlying problem from the real world and defines it as a graphical representation. UML is non-proprietary and not associated with any particular language, methodology or platform.

The main benefit of using UML is that it can provide a common 'language' across business and IT personnel. It also benefits from having many tools that can be used to create and manage the diagramming techniques.

Find more information about UML and all the diagramming techniques at www.uml.org

The first technique I will cover in this section is use cases which describe what a system does from the standpoint of an external observer. Use cases are helpful for a developer because they help them understand who their users are and the boundaries of a system – what is included and what is excluded. Use case diagrams are descriptions of what happens when someone or something interacts with a system.

A use case is described as one use of a system by an actor. An actor is who or what initiates the events involved in a task. Actors are simply roles that people, other systems, organisations or objects play. In UML, communications are the lines that link actors to use case processes and use case processes are shown as ovals. In diagramming use cases, actors are usually shown as stick figures, although this does not mean they are always people (see Figure 3.7).

Figure 3.7 UML use case symbols

Actors are outside the model; they show and set the boundary of what is inside the system and what is outside the system. If they start a use case they are described as active (or primary), if they react to a use case they are described as passive. Examples of actors could include a customer or a bank; Figure 3.8 shows an example for an ATM (automated teller machine).

Figure 3.8 UML use case for an ATM

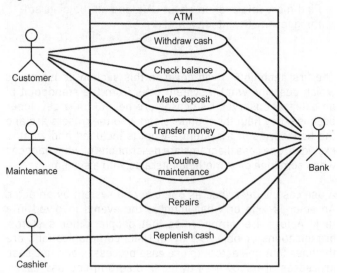

58

Use case diagrams may be helpful in determining features and/or requirements. New use cases may generate new requirements as the system is analysed and the design takes shape. Developers can use use cases to understand and question what the requirements for a new project are really asking for.

As well as the diagramming technique for use cases you can also describe them textually. Use cases can be textually documented in several ways, these include:

- brief – a one-paragraph summary;
- casual – multiple paragraphs that cover a variety of scenarios;
- fully dressed – all steps and variations written in detail.

You may also need to define pre-conditions and post-conditions (states the system assumes before and after the use case), and alternative actions due to exception conditions (errors). The example in Table 3.2 shows a 'casual' text description of a use case.

Table 3.2 Casual text description for a use case

Use case name	Check balance
Actor	Customer
Brief description	This use case describes the way a customer finds out what the current balance of their account is
Flow of events	The customer puts their bank card into the ATM
	The ATM requests the PIN
	The customer enters their PIN for that card/account

(Continued)

Table 3.2 (Continued)

Use case name	Check balance
	The ATM displays a list of available functions
	The customer selects Balance Enquiry
	The ATM displays the option for screen display or printed balance
	The customer chooses either screen display or printed balance
	The ATM outputs the customer's account balance in the selected format
Exception conditions	• If the customer does not provide a valid card no balance is shown and an error message is displayed.
	• The customer can have a maximum of three tries to enter the correct PIN, if after that the PIN is still incorrect the card is ejected and an error message is displayed.
Pre-conditions	The customer has a bank account
Post-conditions	None
Special requirements	None

User stories

User stories are a technique used widely in requirements elicitation and modern software development methodologies such as Agile/Scrum. They are simple to read, concise and widely supported by tools for creation and management. They also benefit from being text-based, so no diagramming is needed.

Just describing what something looks like or what a process does isn't enough for a complete understanding of a process. For example, try the following activity with your team.

Give everyone in the group 30 seconds to write down or draw, or find an image that would represent what comes to mind when you read out this list:

- red;
- four wheels;
- turbo engine;
- stylish looks.

It is likely that some of the people in the group mention a sports car, maybe even a particular make and model of sports car, but not everyone will have had the same idea in mind. In answer to this question I have had some surprising replies including Massey Ferguson tractors and Henry vacuum cleaners. People's answer to this will be based on empiricism; that is, their previous experience and their current knowledge. Not that I'm suggesting people in this example have tractors or particular sports cars, only that they know of their existence and have probably seen them before.

In order to ensure that the product that is built meets the users' ideas and not those of the developer it is necessary to capture the users' needs or goals in some way. One way of doing this that is very popular in Agile development practices is via user stories.

User stories are usually created by the users (or someone writing on the users' behalf) and are used by developers to understand what the users' needs are. User stories are about the users' goals, not system functionality.

The user story format is simple:

As an [actor], I want to [action], so that [goal]

For example: As a consumer, I want a shopping basket so that I can group all my purchases together and pay for them in one go.

As is the case for use cases, an [actor] is a person, system, object or organisation that interacts with the [action] or requirement you describe. The [goal] is the context for the [action] and helps the developer understand the place and importance of the action being described. In short, user stories tell you Who, What and Why.

You should end up with many variations on the same story, from the point of view of different users (stakeholders) as not all users of the system have the same goals. Following on from the user story example above, consider online shopping and the concept of the 'shopping basket'. In addition to the customer perspective we also have these:

- As a warehouse worker, I want a shopping basket so that I can group together all the items for one customer and put them all in the same delivery box.

- As a member of the marketing team, I want a shopping basket so I can see which items a customer buys together which will allow me to build special offer bundles in order to sell more products.

The different user needs expressed in each story tell you a little bit more about what the system is going to be used for and what it needs to do.

User stories explain what a system needs to do from the user's point of view, additional information may be added to them by the developers and product owners when they are being collated into a product backlog. For a product backlog, as a minimum, each story should have:

- A name or identifier.

- A paragraph describing the story (the 'As an [actor] ...' part).

- An indication of the relative importance of this particular story to the actor (there are lots of techniques for this, you could use High, Medium or Low ratings, a simple 1 to 5 numbering system or a technique called MoSCoW which stands for Must have, Should have, Could have, Won't have this time). This prioritisation is necessary so that you can build the most important features into the software first.

- Acceptance criteria, which tell you when the story you are developing is finished, a really important detail for the developer because it lets you know what the feature must do or be in order for you to stop working on it.

The collection of user stories is grouped and prioritised and builds up to provide a list (in the product backlog in Agile/ Scrum) of the features that the application needs to provide. We use the user stories as a basis for estimating the development work required. As developers we also use user stories as the basis for asking questions, planning and managing the development of the system.

User stories are often described by means of the 3Cs:

- Card (because user stories were originally written on index cards):

  - describe who, what and why (the story purpose);

  - describe business value and relative importance;

  - 'promise for a conversation' – the story is a place marker for a conversation to come in which you can find out more about the story.

- Conversation (because the user story is a starting point, more questions and discussions will come later):

  - a conversation is how you get more detail;

  - conversation will likely be ongoing.

- Confirmation:

  - this is the acceptance criteria (how you know it is finished).

One important detail about user stories is their size; you do not need to find out every single detail about the story up front. This is because you only spend time finding out all the finer details nearer the time you are ready to code that functionality. This prevents you spending time on items that may never be included in the final product.

I am of the opinion that all items relating to software development should be represented as some form of user story or otherwise added to the product backlog. This includes the hardware and software setup, ordering items required for the build, plus dependencies, focus group discussions, change requests and bug fixes. This enables time to be properly allocated and logged for all items relating to the product development.

Table 3.3 User story example

Story card

Story ID/Name	1. Grass cutting
As a	gardener
I want	a new tool that allows me to mow my lawn
So that	I can mow my lawn faster than my current manual lawn mower
Priority	Must have
Size	
Author	JC

Acceptance criteria

1	Must be able to mow 1 acre of level lawn in 1 hour or less

In order to create the story shown in Table 3.3 in the product backlog I would have the following:

Card (created by my user, the gardener):

As a gardener I want a new tool that allows me to mow my lawn faster than my current manual lawn mower.

Conversation (questions the developer asked):

Questions to ask would include:

- How big is your lawn?
- Is your lawn level or on a slope?
- How long does it take you to mow your lawn currently?
- What do you mean by faster? Do you have a minimum timespan or percentage improvement in mind?

Confirmation (acceptance criteria derived from the answers to the questions above)

- Must be able to mow 1 acre of level lawn in 1 hour or less.

The end product: based on the user story above I could build a variety of solutions to this problem; I could fix a manual lawn mower to a bicycle frame, I could build a little sit-on mower like a mini tractor, or I could automate the process entirely by building a robotic lawn mower. As a developer I could suggest solutions such as these based on the user's capabilities, my skill as a developer and of course the money and time available for product development.

Cross-platform development

Many traditional programs are intended to run on one particular platform, for example they may be intended for a PlayStation 3 or a PC running Microsoft Windows. Some types of modern development are expected to be cross-platform (for webpages the term used is 'responsive'). This could mean that one program is written in such a way that it will work and adapt across multiple platforms; an example of this would be a webpage that will work on desktop, laptop, tablet and mobile phone platforms in a variety of browsers running on those platforms (this could be done in several ways, for example by changing the layout and style of the page by altering image size, menu format or display height or width). Alternatively, a cross-platform program could have several versions, each of which is aimed at a particular platform but can share some code in common. The most challenging scenario is that a program is written to run on different platforms in different languages. An example of this would be a mobile app written in Objective-C to run on iOS and written in Java to run on Android. This may have occurred when a native app was originally written for Android (in Java); if the same app was then needed for iOS, Java would not work so a new version of the app would be needed in a different language (Objective-C).

As a developer you will be expected to understand how to make your programs cross-platform if necessary. One of the key considerations when you get requirements is to make sure you know which platforms the product should run on.

Understanding and ensuring quality

Software **quality** is all about fitness for purpose. Providing a product that is of the highest quality will help to ensure a good user experience and should also mean that any ongoing support for that product is as easy as is possible. When you are developing a product, you should ask these basic questions:

- Does it do what is needed?
- Does it do it in the way that its users need it to?
- Does it do it reliably enough? Fast enough? Safely enough? Securely enough?
- Will it be affordable?

- Will it be ready when its users need it?
- Can it be changed as needs change?

Three important areas that will help you to improve software quality are **standards**, **good development practices** and **testing**. Let's start with standards.

Standards
The definition, availability and consistent use of standards within your company or organisation should help you ensure:

- that software meets certain pre-defined criteria including testing, documentation and coding style;
- that developers understand how software should be structured and built;
- that software is built in such a way that everyone who works on it should be able to maintain it into the future with a minimum amount of effort deciphering its structure, meaning, logic or naming standards;
- that systems are built to a certain quality level.

As important as having standards is ensuring that people have access to them, understand what they are and why the organisation has them and, crucially, follow them. As a developer you should find out about the standards applicable to your company. Ask these questions before you start to code:

- Do you already have company or organisational standards?
- Does everyone know about them?
- Where are they kept?
- Is training available?
- Are they appropriate and up to date?
- Have you considered using techniques that promote and support standards, such as pair programming or mentoring?

Pair programming is a technique where two people work on the same piece of code. It can be difficult to convince a company to use this technique as they often only see two people producing one piece of work instead of two people producing two pieces of work. There are some real benefits to the technique though, for example:

- There are likely to be fewer interruptions. People are less inclined to interrupt two people when they are working together than they are to interrupt one person.

- Enables you to better focus on the code. If you are working with someone else you will usually focus on a task for longer (and be less side tracked by things such as mobile phones or getting lost down a rabbit hole in your favourite search engine).

- Built-in peer review (a testing technique, see the next section for more detail) and checking adherence to standards.

- Good for mentoring or bringing new team members up to speed.

- Good for the 'lottery win scenario' (previously known as the 'under the bus scenario') – if a section of code is worked on and maintained solely by one person, what happens if that person leaves the company? With pair programming you can always ensure at least two people understand each part of the code base.

- Good for ideas exchange, two heads are better than one.

- Can be used to build the tests at the same time as the code. This technique is commonly used in Test Driven Development (TDD) in which the tests are written before the code.

> If you are going to do pair programming make sure you read up on how to do it properly; like all techniques, there are good and bad practices you should be aware of.

There are many organisations that can provide you with standards that have been defined, refined and validated over the years, there are just a few listed here:

- ISO International Organization for Standardization: https://www.iso.org/standards.html

- BSI British Standards Institution: https://shop.bsigroup.com/Browse-By-Subject/ICT---Information-and-Communications-Technology-/

- IEEE Software Engineering Standards, the Institute of Electrical and Electronic Engineering, Inc.: https://www.computer.org

- ANSI American National Standards Institute: https://www.ansi.org

- Accessibility advice and standards: https://www.abilitynet.org.uk/ or https://www.w3.org/WAI/intro/aria

Good development practices
The quality of source code has the biggest impact when it comes to maintaining your applications after initial deployment. The quality of code can be impacted by several things, these include:

- During development:
  - ease of testing and debugging;
  - types and number of formal tests done;
  - the structure of the source code.
- At run time:
  - low resource consumption (memory, CPU, network);
  - security;

69

- robustness – error or fault handling;
- functionality;
- false feature rich additions (discussed later in this section).

- Future work:
  - readability;
  - maintainability;
  - ease of modification or extensibility;
  - portability;
  - supportability.

In the book *Refactoring: Improving the Design of Existing Code* by Martin Fowler with Kent Beck (2019),[1] the following factors for quality code are suggested: robustness, performance, consistency and readability.

In the book it suggests that there are common factors that make code hard to work with and modify. These are:

- programs that are hard to read;
- programs that have duplicated logic;
- programs that require additional behaviour that requires you to change running code: for example, external configurations or settings;
- programs with complex conditional logic.

As well as considering the standards that are used by your company or business sector, there are also some common sense software development good practices that can be applied in order to avoid some of the items in the above list:

- Improve readability:
  - Format code neatly – use tabs and indents to show the relationships of code within the structure.

- Use comments where necessary; make code readable. In the book *Code Complete*, Steve McConnell (2004) states:

  Good code is its own best documentation. As you're about to add a comment, ask yourself, 'How can I improve the code so that this comment isn't needed?'

- Use naming standards for programs, fields and subroutines, for example Hungarian notation is a popular standard.

• Use procedures, functions or subroutines to structure the code (in other words, modularise the code; break it down into 'chunks'). This can also support the DRY principle – **don't repeat yourself**, which helps avoid duplicated logic by having one procedure which can be called by other procedures. For example, if you need to check the password that is being used in several places within your code, don't write the same code several times, write it once in a procedure (a separate piece/section of the code) and call that procedure whenever it is needed. You might be able to put this type of useful code into a separate file which other people can use in their code (you can start to build libraries of reusable code).

• Avoid nesting code complexity, loops within loops and multiple levels of nested IF statements.

• Don't trust data; always check its type and availability.

• Avoid using global variables in most cases. (Variables are the sticky notes of the programming world, they hold data temporarily for use at a later time in your code, then they can be thrown away. A global variable is one that can be used anywhere in your program.) They have no access control (any part of your code could change them), they are more difficult to test, they may waste memory resources, and more.

• Find out about the code patterns for your programming language; these are tried and tested styles of coding used to solve specific programming problems or needs. For example, Memoisation (memento) – this pattern stores the values calculated or created by a procedure when it is passed specific information. When the procedure is called it checks to see if the required results have already been stored before running the code to calculate or create a new value. It's useful for times when the calculation may be very long winded or slow, or the procedure may be called many times with the same information.

- Identify and avoid bad practices that may be used when writing code. In development, bad practices are known as 'code smells' or 'anti-patterns'. There are bad practices that are common among all programming languages and bad practices that are specific for a particular language; you should find out what they are for your programming language.

- Build robust code. Robust software is written in such a way that it does not break easily, and it should recover quickly from, or hold up well under exceptional circumstances. This can be implemented by extensive and effective error handling, data checking, the use of programming patterns, damage confinement and treating faults in such a way that the program can provide continuation.

Software quality may also be improved by what you leave out. In development there is a concept called '**false feature rich**'; in its simplest terms it means giving the user more than they asked for. You might be adding in extra functional capabilities, multiple ways of doing the same thing (via menus or buttons), even providing configuration capabilities for the end user. If you are adding anything to your product that has not been asked for this has the potential to reduce the quality. You might be wondering why that is, but consider the following:

- time taken to code the extras;
- time taken to properly test the extras;
- additional code base to maintain and support;
- additional lines of code loaded into memory at run time;
- more time to do the documentation of the extras;
- more 'things' that could go wrong.

72

These are just from the developer's point of view; there are also potential downsides from the end user's point of view:

- more time to learn the new product;

- more documentation to get through;

- lots of things that they don't use;

- cost: for example 'I paid x amount for this and I don't use half of it';

- later delivery.

Testing and debugging

Testing and debugging are important responsibilities for software developers. Debugging is an informal thing that you do as you go along – 'Does the code run?' if not, change a line of code or two, and try it again – as opposed to formal testing which is planned, documented and repeatable. Formal testing is sometimes automated as well, with products being available that allow you to script the tests to run against your software.

Good testing is part of the quality standard for development, Figure 3.9 shows a broad overview of testing types in development. These comprise:

- Peer review: you can peer review any artefact within the system, for example code or database design. These can be examined by someone with a view to checking various aspects of the artefact. This could include checking for style, standards compliance, readability, robustness etc.

- Walkthrough: a formal meeting that takes the attendees through the product being examined, with a view to finding any anomalies, exchanging ideas and discussing implementation.

- Inspections: a form of peer review, used specifically to identify defects.

- Black box testing: looking at what the product does (its behaviour) and whether its behaviour meets the requirements. Black box (a.k.a. behavioural testing) often examines two different types of behaviour: functional (this is the part everyone thinks about when testing, the part where the tests check to see if the functionality that is required of the product actually works) and non-functional (broadly speaking, this tests to see if the product does what it does well; more on this later in the chapter).

• White box testing: looking at how the product does what it does (its structure). This technique looks at the way the code is built; some of this work can often be automated via products such as 'linters',[2] which are applications that check your code for build quality standards. They look for things such as code smells and poor programming style.

Figure 3.9 Overview of testing in development

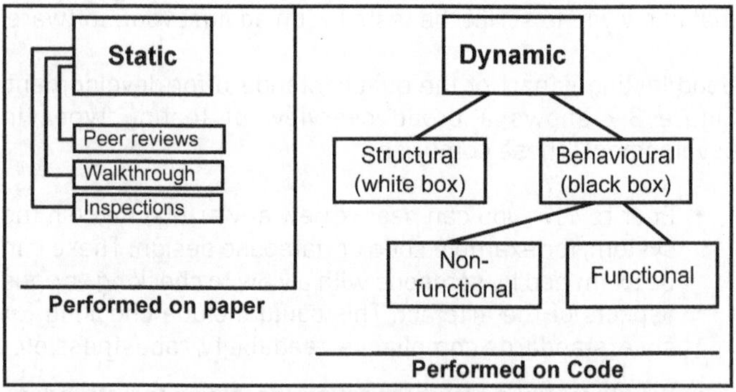

A developer is expected to test the code that they write and each company and domain will have standards for what testing is required. Table 3.4 shows some of the types of testing that would normally be considered for a system or product. Note that this is not an exhaustive list and a developer would not necessarily be expected to cover all of the testing types listed in the table; however it is normally expected that a developer does at least unit testing.

Table 3.4 Description of key testing types that can be run on software

Testing types	Software object being tested	Test objectives
Unit testing	Individual software component, for example a line of code, function, subroutine or procedure	Confirm the component meets its specification
Integration testing	Group of functions, modules or programs which make up part of an application	Ensure that modules which have been individually unit tested can be linked together, that data and control can be passed correctly between them and that they continue to work
	Or a whole system	Check that the system interfaces correctly with other internal systems and ensure that the system interfaces correctly, at both control and data levels, with external systems
System testing	Application segment or whole system	Test that the system fulfils the requirements, both functional and non-functional as per the specification
User acceptance testing	Whole system	Ensure that the system meets the acceptance criteria of the business

(Continued)

Table 3.4 (Continued)

Testing types	Software object being tested	Test objectives
Regression testing	Whole or part of system	Ensure that parts of the application or system which have not been directly changed, continue to operate successfully after other changes have been made

Testing in development usually focuses on verification where you are matching the product to the requirements specification. Other areas of testing that you may be called upon to either understand or participate in in your role as a developer may include the following:

- Validation – matching the product to the business need. Looking at whether the goals of the product's users are being met (earlier in the chapter we looked at user stories; this type of testing would check that the product helps the user in the way they need it to and in accordance with user stories).

- Error centric – concentrating on known problem areas (often known as 'sad path'), checking to make sure the product is robust, whether it deals with errors and if it deals with them well (as opposed to just crashing).

- Benefit directed – concentrating on testing important business areas. This can have a lot of crossover with validation testing.

- Independent testing – not tested by the software writer (testing could be done by a separate test team or another developer).

- Destructive – test simulating environmental problems, also known as load testing or stress testing; for example, this could be testing to see how many people could try to buy products on your ecommerce site at the same time.

- TDD – test driven development (see Chapter 5 for more on this).

- BDD – behaviour driven development (see Chapter 5 for more on this).

Look for information about testing the specific languages you are using. For example, a website and course about testing JavaScript by Kent C. Dodds: https://testingjavascript.com/

Maintenance and refactoring

In Chapter 2 I mentioned that you could well spend some time as a developer maintaining an existing code base. This could be a code base that you have written, or one developed by someone else. The types of maintenance tasks could involve bug fixing for problems that have been found after the code was released; adding enhancements to the product; or changing the code to keep up with changes in the business, law or requirements.

When code is changed you should still maintain all the standards mentioned earlier, that is, software development, company, business sector and legal standards, and ensure the updated code is tested. If the code was developed with a complete set of formal tests initially, these should still be available as a starting point for your regression test runs.

Whenever software is revisited there may be an opportunity for **refactoring**, which is improving the code base. Refactoring could be making the code more efficient, better structured, commented, more readable or otherwise improving the general quality of the code. If a need for refactoring has been identified but not acted upon, these change requirements then become (known as) **technical debt**. Any technical debt identified (but not addressed) on a product is bad, it suggests the code base is not as good as it could be and is often the result of poorly designed or poorly constructed code. As a developer you are very likely to be involved with refactoring code on which technical debt has been identified.

Martin Fowler (2019) has written an excellent book on the subject of refactoring, *Refactoring: Improving the Design of Existing Code*.

Documentation

As a developer you will generally be expected to do some documentation on the products you work on. If you use an Agile approach then this is often done for each item in a sprint and makes up part of a '**definition of done**'; that is, the conditions something must meet in order to be deemed 'complete'. Even if you are not working in an Agile style, you might still find it easier to document as you go along while what you have done is still fresh in your mind. The types of documentation needed will, of course, vary from one product and company to the next.

Various types of documentation may be needed for a product, these could include a **user guide** to show the user how to use the product or a **run book** which describes (usually for administrators) what the system setup is and how to keep the product running 'normally', possibly also containing instructions for error handling, for example a reset or reboot. You may have a **technical specification**, which could include details of (optionally hardware as well as) the software build including data sources and any complex algorithms. Formal testing will have documentation, usually in the form of a **testing plan** plus details of types and levels of testing; this may also document a test run script. You may also have a **data dictionary**, which explains all the types of data used in the system including their data types, ranges and sizes with examples of valid data for each. There will also be documentation produced earlier in the SDLC as mentioned previously in the book, for example the user stories.

Other items you may be expected to document include:

- units of measurement used;
- for external or third-party products or libraries which you use in your code, documentation that explains what it is, how to use it, problems, pitfalls and examples of use;
- a quick reference guide;
- database schemas.

Consideration of non-functional requirements

When most developers and systems specialists start looking at a new product they focus on what it will do; that is, the functionality. End users are looking at the product as a whole, not only what it does (the functionality) but also how it does it (the NFRs, non-functional requirements), including such variables as ease of use, response speed, cost, reliability, accessibility and so on. When developing a system, or modifying or augmenting it, you should consider these additional (non-functional) requirements.

There are various approaches to remembering, including and evaluating NFR within a system: the FURPS+ acronym is helpful, or there is the ISO/IEC/IEEE 25010:2011 standard (https://www.iso.org/standard/35733.html) which covers product quality standards (not just NFR).

FURPS+ is an acronym originating at HP (Hewlett Packard) by Robert Grady and Deborah L. Caswell. It is used as a reminder of **software quality attributes**. The characters stand for:

- **Functionality** – this is the actions and capabilities of the product: what the product can do.
- **Usability** – this looks at user interface considerations such as ease of use, aesthetics and consistency.

> This can be a role in its own right: UX (User eXperi-ence) designer or UX engineer. There are also for-mal scientific roles that deal solely with the user interface. These are (predominantly known in the UK as) graphical user interface (GUI) designers and (predominantly an American role) human factors analysts (Hufa) who all work in this area.

- **Reliability** – this is concerned with how much up-time (the amount of time that a product runs without stopping for some reason) the product has and how easy it is to recover when something happens.

- **Performance** – how well the product performs its tasks. This could be looking at areas such as processing speed, how quickly the product responds when given a task, how long it takes for the product to be ready to use when it is switched on or started up, or how quickly the product can recover when something goes wrong.

- **Supportability** – how easy a product is to support. This can cover areas such as how easy it is to change the way the product is configured or set up, how easy it is to service the product: for example provide updates or changes to the way the product works.

- The + part both supports and enhances the requirements mentioned above with four extra areas for consideration:

  - Design requirements – this covers constraints or limitations on the way the product is built, how the software works (for example the webpage must run over https), what legal restrictions may be put on it (for example GDPR), and platform-based considerations (for example what browsers it must run on).

  - Implementation requirements – standards on how it is built (for example it must have Welsh language support).

- Interface requirements – requirements to other systems or the system this product will work within; in other words, how this product works with existing or planned systems already in use on the platform.

- Physical requirements – hardware or environmental.

The NFRs mentioned in FURPS+ fall into two types, constraint-based and quality-based NFR. Constraint-based types are typically not subject to negotiation; examples might include legal or industry regulation adherence, platform-based constraints such as hardware, operating system, programming language or database restrictions. These types of constraint are often easier to test, for example, does the product run on iOS?

Quality-based NFR can be more difficult as they are often subjective, what's 'easy to use' for you might be difficult for someone else. They can be difficult to test. There are three ways to test quality-based NFR:

- An actual test: for example, 'it needs to be fast', with a response of under 3 seconds; that would give you an actual test – 'the response time is 3 seconds or less'.

- A proxy test: this is a representation that all stakeholders agree represents the requirement. For example, for the requirement 'it needs to be easy to use', your representative test could be – 'it should be less than six clicks from initial menu click to task completion' or 'usable by a complete novice without guidance within (a stated time)'. The key thing to remember here is that all the stakeholders need to agree, so a discussion is needed to come up with ideas and an agreement.

- A 'shows best efforts' test: this is by far the 'loosest' and most difficult of the testing types. Take a NFR of 'easy to support'. You can develop the product in ways that provide good supportability, for example, robust and well-structured code, meaningful error messages and so on, but until you actually have to support the product you cannot be sure if it's easy or not. This type of test could track metrics for an existing product, looking at the number of problems in a given time period, level of support needed (1st line, 2nd line etc.) and how the problem was fixed (code change, configuration, re-boot etc.). You could then track the same metrics over the same timescale in the new product and compare the two sets of results.

You should always take the list given by FURPS+ as your starting point but there may be many other NFR that your company uses in its products. See if there is a working list (if not, why not offer to create one, it could become the company standard).

The standards mentioned above give the following suggestions for NFR:

ISO/IEC/IEEE 25010:2011 contains eight NFR (which contain subgroups, not listed here), these are: Functional suitability, Performance efficiency, Compatibility, Usability, Reliability, Security, Maintainability and Portability.

Security

For those that have access to it, the internet has changed everything: so many aspects of our lives use the internet. One of the main areas of change is the availability of data; having the ability to look something up and get a fairly instantaneous response is a very useful thing but in terms of security it comes at a cost. So many more people, including criminals, have access to data and the networks that your application's data may use. There are cyber threats, hackers, denial of service attacks, viruses, trojans, worms and more, not to mention loss of network connectivity. As part of a robust security strategy you should consider the following:

- Risk analysis of common security threats, for example:
  - human error (add robust error handling to help protect your program);

- un-patched vulnerabilities in both the operating system and hardware (check the vulnerabilities that have been found and add the recommended patches or code);
- external threats such as hackers;
- unsanctioned network access.
- Keeping known security threats in mind as you code. See:
  - OWASP top ten (https://www.owasp.org);
  - Dictionary of Software Weakness Types (http://cwe.mitre.org/top25).
- Carrying out a software weakness review to show that you have thought about potential weakness, for example on:
  - management of credentials;
  - admin;
  - logging sensitive information;
  - persistence and storage of sensitive data.
- Requesting a security audit. There may be a team in your company that can do this or you can employ white hat hackers to do it for you.

> Some of the companies that produce anti-virus software have regular competitions where they pay people who can find vulnerabilities in their anti-virus code. Other companies run 'ethical hacker' competitions where they give prizes to people who expose vulnerabilities in their company computer systems.

- Taking a course on cyber security. You can often find free online courses on cyber security available through websites such as FutureLearn (www.futurelearn.com).

Functional requirements or NFRs may highlight security issues. These are often system-wide concerns and you will need to communicate and collaborate with your team in order to make sure you apply security consistently across all areas of the product. They may be applicable in multiple places (possibly using multiple techniques), in different ways and at different levels: for example logging in to a gateway, authorisation to access a specific type of function (for example an administrator role), authority to view data or secure backup of data, physical security or logging restrictions.

For the language you use and the business sector you work in you will need to know what security threats are present and how to code and test against them.

INTERFACE AND DEPENDENCIES

The last part of this chapter looks at the other roles you might meet as a developer; it is helpful to understand this so you can ask the right questions of the right people when necessary. Definitions shown here are from the SFIA documentation in the systems development category so bear in mind that the people you work with may not fit these lists exactly.

It is also helpful to understand associated roles should you be looking to move from a developer role into another area within systems development. There may be other aspects of your work that you particularly enjoy, for example the analysis role or testing; if that is the case these descriptions can give you an insight into new fields of study and possible role migration opportunities.

Recognising the other roles in systems development

When you are working as part of a team or with other people involved in the product development it is a good idea to find out what the people you work with do.

A note about semantics, the skills or roles described in this section are not necessarily job titles; they may be, but equally they can describe part of a job covered by one or more people.

The SFIA framework[3] mentioned in Chapter 1 outlines some roles within system development. I will briefly summarise those role titles in this section. This will not be a definitive list of all the other roles you may work with in product development; you may well work with end users or other stakeholders for your product, but this gives you a starting point.

- **Systems development management** – responsible for overall planning for the product, this can include budgets, quality standards and timescales as well as identifying resources. It is also likely that the person in this role will decide what management methodology or approach will be used for the SDLC. From the developer's point of view the person in this role has a management position and it is likely that you will need to report to them.

- **Systems design** – the systems designer will be responsible for deciding the overall architecture of the product, ensuring it meets the requirements and quality standards plus any technical constraints imposed for the system. They may be responsible for creating some of the designs and plans mentioned in this chapter (ERD and use cases) that are used by the developer to understand the systems requirements.

- **Software design** – responsible for the specification and design of the software to meet defined requirements. They may decide what software development patterns will be used and will help with design decisions in areas such as non-functional requirements. People in this role will help the developer to ensure they build good quality code.

- **Real-time or embedded systems development** – people in this role will be responsible for the architecture, design and development of reliable, real-time software, operating systems, tools and embedded systems. This is a developer role; you may work in a team that creates software of this type or you may write this type of software yourself.

- **Animation development** – as the name suggests, animation developers will be responsible for the architecture, design and development of animated and interactive systems such as games and simulations. If you work on games development you may have this role or you may work with others that do this.

- **Data modelling and design** – responsible for the investigation, evaluation, interpretation and modelling of data, in order to define, communicate and clarify information structures and data. Professionals in this area may be responsible for creating some of the designs and plans mentioned in this chapter (ERD) that are used by the developer in order to understand data requirements.

- **Database design** – the person in this role will generally design, build and maintain the databases or file storage on the product platform. People in this role may help the developer with data access via SQL.

- **Network design** – responsible for strategies, architecture, documentation and design of networks of any kind (for example the email system as well as a physical computer network). If you are working on software that runs across a network the people in this role may be able to help a developer understand and use the network requirements specific to their product.

- **Testing** – planning, design, management, execution and reporting of tests, using appropriate testing tools and techniques. Software testers may work with developers in pair programming or may test the work developers' products, or both.

- **Safety engineering** – using appropriate methods to assure safety during all life cycle phases of safety-related systems developments; this includes risk analysis, safety requirements, maintenance and re-use.

- **Information content authoring** – a content management role responsible for designing, authoring, controlling and presenting text-based information, for example the text displayed on a website.

Roles in Agile/Scrum

In addition to the SFIA roles and skills listed in this section there are three roles which are part of Agile/Scrum development. These are Product Owner, Dev Team and Scrum Master, all of which were briefly described in Chapter 2. A developer would be part of the dev team.

To find out more about all of these roles please see *The Scrum Guide* (Schwaber and Sutherland, 2017).[4]

SUMMARY

In this chapter we have explored some of the key skills needed for the role of software developer. These are logical (or analytical) thinking, knowledge of a programming language and an understanding of data.

We also looked at some of the (possible) responsibilities for a developer, noting that the actual list may vary depending on context and company, but in general you will need to understand the requirements, undertake cross-platform development, work on standards, quality and testing and have a good understanding of non-functional requirements and security concerns for your domain.

Finally, we briefly considered some of the roles undertaken by other possible members of your team, department or company.

The next chapter looks at some key programming concepts and looks at the programming languages you could use. It also introduces the types of products those languages could be used to create.

4 PROGRAMMING LANGUAGES

First, solve the problem. Then, write the code.

John Johnson

One of the main skills for a developer is using programming languages. This chapter will cover a variety of popular languages and explain the key and common uses for that language, the sectors or products in which the languages are most prevalent, and give brief examples of what the language looks like, and what might prompt a developer to use that language. I will also suggest some additional learning resources for each language.

The language chosen by the developer will drive the types of product that the developer works on and you will need to learn (at least) one of the languages commonly used to build the type of product you are interested in developing. For example, if you want to develop webpages you will need to learn HTML, CSS and JavaScript.

In general, the FutureLearn website (www.futurelearn.com) has some great free online courses from some of the top universities in the UK and across the world. The courses are free at the time of writing but if you want a certificate of completion you will need to pay for that.

Another great resource for free online courses is Udemy (https://www.udemy.com/) which contains some competitively priced online courses. When you search for the subject in Udemy set the search filter to free to just see the free courses. I won't specifically mention either of these two sites in the further reading for each language, but you should check them for all languages.

As well as courses there are also community and social sites that can help to teach and mentor new developers. See Chapter 6 for more details.

DEVELOPMENT PRACTICES

First, let's look at some development practices relating to languages that you may have heard of: high and low level, object oriented, event driven, procedural, functional, open source, libraries and frameworks. It is important that software developers understand what these terms mean.

High level, low level

When developing a program or a system the code can be described as low level (this is machine language, for example, binary) or high level (this is human readable code and is the most popular way of writing software).

Programs written in high level languages are often **compiled**. This means that a compiler program translates the code into machine readable language. The compiler creates a separate file, which is the actual file you run on the device (not the code the developer writes). You write in a high level language and the compiler translates it into a low level language that the computer can run.

Some languages such as JavaScript, which is used in the production of most webpages, are **interpreted**; this means that when they are running the program that interprets them (for example a browser), they will parse a line (read and check the line of code is valid) then execute the line of code. Interpreted languages tend to run slower than compiled languages; they do not go through a compile stage.

If you work with JavaScript already you might hear the word **transpile** (a combination of transform and compile). Some tools will run your code through this stage; this changes the code from what you have written to another format. The benefit of this transpile stage is that you can use a library (pre-written code) or another language, for example TypeScript, to develop your webpage and the transpiler will convert that into JavaScript for you. Transpiled code is still human readable; it is not machine code.

In web development, libraries such as babel and languages such as TypeScript or Coffeescript can provide a simpler (and often more robust and easily maintainable) syntax than writing in JavaScript.

Object oriented

Think about an ecommerce website. When you are using the site you deal with products, orders, delivery options, payment options and doubtless many other things too numerous to list here. Each of the things I just listed, for example an order, is a discrete (self-contained, individually separate) item in the system. In object oriented systems, each discrete item is known as an object. So you would have an order object, a product object and so on.

An object oriented (OO) programming language is one that is based around the concept of objects. Examples of OO languages are Java, Python, Ruby, C#, C++, Smalltalk and Objective-C, to name but a few. Objects are said to **encapsulate** the data and functionality relating to the object. Let's cover the basic terminology first.

The template (known as a **class**) for an order would describe all the functionality (**methods**) and data (**properties or attributes**) relating to all types of order, irrespective of who made them or what they contained.

Figure 4.1 Object oriented: a few of the methods and properties for an order

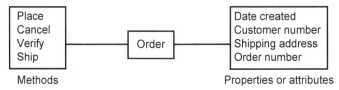

| Methods | | Properties or attributes |

Figure 4.1 shows an example of some of the methods and properties for an order, although in reality there would be more than this; when you build your ecommerce site you would design the order object with everything you thought it needed.

When you create an **instance** of a class, you create an **object**.

When I buy something on an ecommerce site, the application will create a new order for me; it will create a new instance of an order object. That object **inherits** all the methods and properties of its class, which means I can place an order or cancel an order etc. and the application will create an order number, store my customer number, shipping address and the date I placed the order.

SUMMARY OF TERMINOLOGY

- **Class**: a template for something.
- **Method**: something that can be done by an object (a function).
- **Property**: (also known as an attribute) a piece of data relating to an object.
- **Object**: an instance of a defined class.
- **Instance**: a copy of a class, an instance of a class is called an object.

- **Inheritance**: an object can use the methods and properties defined by its class; it inherits them.

- **Encapsulation**: the concept of an object containing its data and the methods that can be used to read or change that data. In the order example, there is a property called customer number, the order class would have methods to access that property, possibly called GetCustomerNumber and SetCustomerNumber.

If you translate this paradigm to development you could design a class for a window (one on the computer). You could try that now, and consider what functionality is available for a window – for example 'Open'. What about the data? Size perhaps?

What other methods and properties could you have in your window class?

The easiest way to do this is to think about how you interact with a window on the computer. You start the program and the window **opens**, it displays the initial (home) page plus perhaps a menu? You could **scroll** up and down on the page and usually **move** the screen to a new **position** or **resize** it. When you have finished with it you will **close** the window (see Figure 4.2). Consider the words in bold; which are actions (methods) and which are information (properties)?

Figure 4.2 Window methods and properties

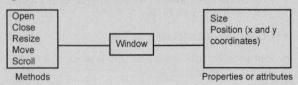

Now take the concept to an application for a bank. Your online banking application could have object classes to describe a customer and an account (there will be more but let's start with those two). The account could have properties for current balance, account type and account number; it could have methods for deposit, withdraw, GetBalance, and more. What other properties and methods can you think of? What about the customer class, what properties and methods could that have?

If you are working with an object oriented language you should spend some time looking at the SOLID principles.[1] They were devised by Robert C. Martin (known as 'Uncle Bob') and are part of good coding standards practice. They provide five guidelines that can help you to design and build better products by focusing on principles that make code more maintainable.

This site has a good explanation of the principles: www.blackwasp.co.uk/SOLID.aspx

Event driven

Unlike object oriented languages designed specifically to work with objects, programming languages are not 'event driven languages'.

Event driven is a way of programming a system so that it responds to things that happen irrespective of the order that they occur in. In programming terms, an event is something that happens in a program, system or application, an action such as a mouse click or a keypress. Event driven programs are ones whose flow of control and process execution is determined by events.

This type of programming can be used in web-based or windows-based programs and often in device driver or sensor-based programs. For example, if you have a timer for a toy car racing set, the event would be the car running under a gantry with a sensor on it; this would cause some code to run which works out how long it had been since the car last went under the sensor. This means that a program is event driven based on its use, not its development language. Event driven applications could also be object oriented; the two concepts are not mutually exclusive.

Procedural

Often seen in contrast to event driven languages, procedural languages follow a series of steps or routines which are carried out in sequence. The sequence can vary depending on variables, data, exceptions or conditions that happen in the program. The procedures (which are known as routines, subroutines or functions, depending on which programming language you use, and for some languages, depending on if the procedure returns a value) can be called by other procedures and can in their turn call more procedures; in programming this is sometimes known as a call stack.

Envisage a program which controls the startup of a device, such as an in-car navigation system. It would run the same sequence of code procedures in order to get it ready to use. If there was a problem with getting the maps (an exception occurred) for instance, it could run error handling, otherwise it would prepare the device for use in the same way every time.

Whether code is procedural or not depends on the application use. In some cases code runs on systems that are not capable of running anything other than procedural code (they cannot for instance run event driven code), so languages designed and used for these systems are procedural languages; an example is IBM's RPG language. Languages such as C could be used to write procedural, and also event driven code.

Functional

To describe a functional programming style I first have to describe a **pure function**; that is, a function which returns a value, the result of which is dependent only on parameters passed into the function and what the function itself does in code (the algorithm). It is important to understand that with this type of function, if you pass the same values in, you will get the same result out every time. These functions do not have any outside influences and are not dependent on the state or values of any outside variables. Pure functions are said to have no side effects, meaning they do not affect anything outside the function; for example, they do not change the values of outside variables or the program's state.

Functional programming is writing code which has pure functions. Some programming languages are designed to be written only in a functional programming style, for example Haskell; other programming languages are compatible with functional programming but do not enforce the style, for example Lisp and Python.

There are many techniques that you can use in functional programming. See Mary Rose Cook's excellent article https://maryrosecook.com/blog/post/a-practical-introduction-to-functional-programming for a fuller explanation with examples using the Python language.

Open source

Something that is described as being open source is publicly accessible; it can be used for free, copied, shared, edited or otherwise modified by its users. There may however be some restrictions on use, for example you may not be able to sell software that you acquired via open source. Each piece of open source software will state what the terms and conditions are. A well-known example of an open source programming language is the PHP programming language.

Useful resources for more on open source are:

https://www.thebalancecareers.com/what-is-open-source-software-2071941

https://opensource.com/resources/what-open-source

Libraries and frameworks

Libraries and frameworks are files providing ready written code which can give extra capabilities, easy to use extensions or syntactic sugar to your programming. Languages like JavaScript have hundreds of different libraries and frameworks contributed by its very large community of users from private individuals to large companies. If you have used JavaScript you may have heard of some of them; popular ones include jQuery, React, Backbone and Bootstrap.

So what is the difference between a library and a framework? A library provides a function or functions that you can use in your code.

A framework provides (dictates) an architecture that your code must adhere to in order to use its functionality; for example Backbone provides an MVC (model view controller) style architecture. Some JavaScript 'libraries' can be used as both a framework and a library.

MVC (model view controller) is a way of designing and building your code so that it has distinct Model (the data), View (the user interface) and Controller (the code that keeps the Model and View correctly synchronised) components. It is an architectural pattern for software development.

THE LANGUAGES

The languages chosen for this chapter were selected because they are either in the Stack Overflow most popular languages list, they are listed in the SFIA guide, or they are languages used to develop some of the types of program mentioned in this book.

The results from the Stack Overflow 2019 survey (https://insights. stackoverflow.com/survey/2019#technology) mentioned earlier in the book gave us this list of popular programming languages (listed here in no particular order):

- JavaScript;
- HTML & CSS;
- SQL;
- Python;
- Java;
- C#;
- PHP;
- C++;
- C;
- Ruby;
- Bash/Shell;
- TypeScript.

And recently sliding down the list – Objective-C, Swift and VB.Net.

In the 1970s and 1980s, you would tend to specialise in one language, for example C, plus other associated languages such as SQL for data access and perhaps a scripting language such as Bash, if your platform needed it. Many developers do start with one language, perhaps moving to a new language to further their career or at their employers' request. It is common now for software developers to be familiar with a few languages.

If you are working on web development, you will need to know HTML, CSS and JavaScript. If you work as a server-side, back-end or full-stack developer (see Chapter 2 for an explanation of these roles), you will need at least one server-side language, for example PHP, Python, C# or Java. Some full-stack or server-side developers use node.js; this is a program (an interpreter) written in C, C++ and JavaScript that lets you use JavaScript on the server side, instead of having to learn and use another language (thus saving you the trouble of having different languages on the client and server). This capability can give rise to a technique called universal (or isomorphic) code; if you have used React on the server side with JavaScript you may be familiar with this.

The languages that will be covered in this chapter are JavaScript, HTML, CSS, SQL, Java, Python, C, C#, PHP, C++ and Ruby. For each language I will suggest some resources for learning; the resources I suggest will be freely available and will be internet-based. You may prefer to go on a paid classroom-based course; if so, you could look at the BCS list of accredited training providers (https://partner.bcs.org/) or access your favourite training provider, or further education resources. Alternatively, you can refer to books (see the further reading list at the end of this book). In the majority of cases the code example shown will output the words 'Hello World'; this is a very simple (and traditional) first application.

JavaScript, HTML, CSS

Key uses
JavaScript, HTML and CSS are (mostly) interpreted[2] languages used in webpage development or mobile app development.

In webpage or app development, these three languages are used as follows:

Content (the text, links and images) is handled using **HTML**.
Style (the appearance and layout) is defined in **CSS**.
Interaction (how it behaves) is controlled using **JavaScript**.

These languages do not have a particular business sector use; their predominance is in developing a certain type of product, namely webpages. The development of webpages, ecommerce and mobile apps has escalated in recent years with the continuing rise in the importance of the internet and the connected society. This is one area where you see real growth in the employment market.

While these languages are best known for webpage development it is possible to use the languages to create native apps (an application that you can download from a mobile app store, for example Google Play or iOS App Store). You develop the app using these languages then use a product such as PhoneGap[3] to make it compatible with the native app requirements for the intended platform. Alternatively you could use something like React Native; this is a JavaScript-based library that lets you build native apps that will work cross-platform on iOS and Android.

You can also build desktop apps using these languages but currently you need a framework to do this, for example Electron[4] or Meteor[5]. See this article for more examples: https://brainhub.eu/blog/javascript-frameworks-for-desktop-apps/

Syntax examples
HTML – define a paragraph with content

```
<p id='mytext'>Hello world</p>
```

CSS – change font size and colour on that paragraph

```
p {
      font-size: 18pt;
      color:blue;
}
```

JavaScript – select the paragraph and override the CSS font colour

```
document.getElementById('mytext').style.
color = 'green';
```

Further resources

There are many sites where you can learn about HTML, CSS and JavaScript; at the time of writing these are some free resources I can recommend:

100 days of code (https://www.100daysofcode.com/): a community of people who are all learning to code and supporting each other in the process.

Free Code Camp (https://www.freecodecamp.org/): this is a US-based site where you can learn to code and get experience by helping not-for-profit organisations.

There are also many sites that can help with standards and reference material for these languages:

The World Wide Web consortium set the standards for web development (https://www.w3.org/).

The HTML5 platform page has links to many other pages with standards and syntax examples (https://platform.html5.org/).

In this book I have mentioned several JavaScript libraries. The libraries and their websites are listed here, most of them have very good tutorials for beginners:

jQuery: https://jquery.com/
React: https://reactjs.org/
React Native: https://facebook.github.io/react-native/
PhoneGap: https://phonegap.com/
Bootstrap: https://getbootstrap.com/
Backbone: https://backbonejs.org/

SQL

Key uses

SQL can be used on its own in a database management system or embedded in code to access database information.

SQL is a CRUD- (Create, Retrieve, Update, Delete) capable language for use with databases. There are many 'flavours' of

SQL – some databases have specific syntax for that database only – there are also generic standards for SQL, for example Transact SQL which works on several manufacturers' database products. SQL may be used by anyone or any organisation that needs to use data from a database.

Syntax examples
A SQL statement used to get all the information on a particular customer record might look like this:

```
SELECT * FROM customer WHERE CustomerID =
123456
```

Further resources
Khan academy has a free course on SQL:
https://www.khanacademy.org/computing/computer-programming/sql

Transact SQL reference: https://docs.microsoft.com/en-us/sql/t-sql/language-reference?view=sql-server-2017

MySQL SQL reference: https://dev.mysql.com/doc/refman/8.0/en/sql-syntax.html

Java

Key uses
Java is a compiled language, and the main language used to create mobile apps that run on Android. It is also widely used to create web-based server-side code. It can be used in cloud-based application development, libraries and frameworks or application programming interfaces (APIs), embedded product development as well as enterprise program development. Java is a good general-purpose language.

Syntax examples
```
class HelloWorldApp {
     public static void main(String[ ] args) {
     System.out.println("Hello World");
}
}
```

Further resources
Beginners guide to Java: https://beginnersbook.com/java-tutorial-for-beginners-with-examples/

Codecademy online course: https://www.codecademy.com/learn/learn-java

Here is a nice quick reference from Princeton: https://introcs.cs.princeton.edu/java/11cheatsheet/

Python

Key uses
Python is a general-purpose, interpreted language which is widely used in web development on the server side, and is a very popular language for teaching programming, often used on products such as the Raspberry Pi. It is also used in the scientific community and for data mining.

In addition to this it can be used as an embedded language and also to create small scripts to run things such as tests.

It has a wide range of pre-made modules available for use that have been written by its extensive user community; the Python software foundation webpage (https://www.python.org/about/apps/) gives more detail on these.

Python can also be used as an extra language by developers, to power automated scripts or to prototype small projects such as sensors or timers. There is a link to success stories at the main Python foundation webpage: https://www.python.org/about/success/

Syntax examples
```
print("Hello World ")
```

Note that this code does exactly the same thing (outputs the string "Hello World") as the code shown in the Java and other language sections.

102

Further resources

Excellent information and resources on the Python wiki page: https://wiki.python.org/moin/FrontPage#start

There are some free Python courses at Data Camp: https://www.datacamp.com/courses/intro-to-python-for-data-science

Everything you need to learn and set up the development environment from the Python Guru: https://thepythonguru.com/

C

Key uses

C as a language is older than the others listed in this chapter and because of that it has wide use across many sectors and a lot of legacy code is out there. It is more often used now in systems programming (writing operating systems, device drivers and embedded software). It is also used to write software that interprets or implements other languages, such as Python.

Syntax examples

```
#include <stdio.h>
int main()
{
 printf("Hello, World!");
 return 0;
}
```

Further resources

While many programming forums will insist that you learn C programming, it is probably not the easiest language to start with. It may be better to learn a less technically challenging language to start with if you have never programmed before. You can practise the use of logic, program planning and basic syntax structures in most languages before you approach C.

A short taster course is available here: https://alison.com/course/introduction-to-c-programming

A free, interactive C tutorial is: https://www.learn-c.org/

A simple beginner project: https://www.makeuseof.com/tag/learn-c-programming-beginner-project/

An American online course, this site also serves as a portal to several other courses in C, at various levels, by the same group: https://www.edx.org/course/c-programming-getting-started

C#

Key uses
Originating in Microsoft's Visual Studio IDE, C# was originally seen as a business-based, application development language (for Windows-based applications). Over time it has gained popularity and now often appears in job adverts commanding good salaries for experienced practitioners.

As well as being a good general-purpose language for application building it is also becoming popular for developing games.

The newest version of C# at the time of writing will let you run applications on non-Windows platforms. Nevertheless it is still mostly used for development of applications intended to run on Windows machines across a variety of sectors, including those building server-side code for the web.

I see a lot of job adverts for this language in the finance, banking and insurance industries.

Syntax examples

```
using System;
namespace HelloWorld
{
 class Hello
 {
 static void Main()
 {
 Console.WriteLine("Hello World!");
 }
 }
}
```

Further resources

Beginners tutorial: https://www.guru99.com/c-sharp-tutorial.html

As a Microsoft product, a great range of reference material for C# can be found on its site: https://docs.microsoft.com/en-us/dotnet/csharp/index

Also see the Microsoft C# tutorials: https://docs.microsoft.com/en-us/dotnet/csharp/tutorials/

PHP

Key uses

A little confusingly, the acronym PHP is now said to stand for Hypertext Pre-processor; originally it was Personal Home Page which gives you some idea of its original intended use by its creator (Rasmus Lerdorf).

Not originally designed as a full programming language, PHP has grown over the years to become a popular server-side development language.

Companies that create server-based web applications or websites can use PHP as their language of choice. Another popular example of its use is by individuals or companies who want to develop WordPress themes, plug-ins or modify the default behaviour of WordPress as PHP is the scripting language used by the site.

Syntax examples

```
<?php
echo '<p>Hello World</p>';
?>
```

This looks like HTML because it is embedded in an HTML file, the <? Syntax is what causes it to run on the server side.

Further resources

The PHP documentation has a good tutorial; it's a great place to start: http://php.net/manual/en/tutorial.php

You can get certification for PHP skills from here: www.zend.com/en/services/certification

PHP tutorial – some basic programming knowledge is needed to use this to its best advantage: https://www.tutorialspoint.com/php/

Good beginner tutorial: https://www.tutorialrepublic.com/php-tutorial/

C++

Key uses
C++ was originally based on the very popular C programming language but with the added advantage of object oriented classes. Enterprise applications, systems software and games development are the main uses for C++. It is the most popular language in the games industry with the class-based object oriented structure making reusability (of code) an achievable goal.

C++ also has a following among developers who take part in programming competitions.

Syntax examples
```
#include <iostream>
using namespace std;
int main()
{
 cout << "Hello, World!";
 return 0;
}
```

Further resources
An easy to follow tutorial on C++: https://www.programiz.com/cpp-programming

Another simple introduction to the language can be found at: www.cplusplus.com/doc/tutorial/

A reference to C++ from the man who developed the language: www.stroustrup.com/C++.html

News and discussions about C++: https://isocpp.org/

An excellent resource including tips on interviews: https://www.geeksforgeeks.org/c-plus-plus/

Beginners tutorial on C++: https://beginnersbook.com/2017/08/c-plus-plus-tutorial-for-beginners/

Ruby

Key uses
Ruby was designed as a general-purpose language and can be used for building desktop applications and games. It is probably best known in web development for Ruby on Rails (a server-side-based web application framework) and Jekyll (a site builder written in Ruby).

Companies that build products that are web-based can use Ruby for server-side development.

Syntax examples
```
puts 'Hello, world!'
```

Further resources
A simple introduction to Ruby is a good place to start: https://www.digitalocean.com/community/tutorials/how-to-write-your-first-ruby-program

There is also a good reference on the Wikibooks site: https://en.wikibooks.org/wiki/Ruby_Programming

The Ruby website's documentation provides some beginner tutorials and setup advice: https://www.ruby-lang.org/en/documentation/

SUMMARY

In this chapter we looked at some of the development practices that you may need, depending on the programming language you use. I also introduced a selection of programming languages in common use for modern development, along with some suggestions for learning those languages. The next chapter looks at some of the work practices you may need for development work in addition to some tools and environments you may encounter or use.

5   TOOLS, METHODS AND TECHNIQUES

> The purpose of software engineering is to control complexity, not to create it.
>
> Pamela Zave

This chapter looks at some of the other tools, environments or work practices that may be involved in programming or that software developers may be required to utilise or include in their role.

THE DEVELOPMENT ENVIRONMENT

Every programming language has different requirements for the environment that you use to create and test your code. This will be based not only on the language you use but also on your platform, both the one you use for development and the one you are intending to deploy the code to. You may use the minimum tools required or you may use a complicated mix of tools and environmental setup in order to develop, test and document the program.

Build tools

As the name suggests, build tools are the tools, products and environments you use to help you create your products. They can range from one or two very simple tools to very elaborate sets of combined products and tools, some of which take quite a long time and some effort to set up. As with all things developer-related, exactly what you need depends on the programming language, the product, the company and the developer, in other words, build tools are to be used in context. Because your choice of tools is context-related, this chapter will give you a broad introduction to the products available to developers and their potential uses; you need to find out which setup is used in your company.

Text editors

The simplest sort of build tools are plain text editors; similar to word processors they provide the simplest way to enter your code onto the computer. An example of a text editor is Microsoft's Visual Studio Code program. They do not add additional things to your code (as integrated development environments (IDEs) may do) but they often have additional 'plug-ins' you can use to make writing code easier.

The one you use generally depends on the operating system and platform you work on, the language you develop in and personal preference. It's good to find a text editor that gives you some basic help by providing (often via plug-ins) the following:

- Support for your programming language, perhaps including language or syntax templates.

- Syntax highlighting (ability to highlight keywords and other syntax in different colours for easy reading).

- Intellisense (dropdown list of keywords to complete the phrase you are writing – great for fast coding and if you can't remember the exact syntax).

- Debugging tools, preferably with single step code line execution and watch capability (the ability to see the contents of your variables and other areas of code change in real time).

- Plug-ins or add-ons for common editing needs, for example spell check, prettifiers (tabs and spaces added to your code to make it more readable) and diffs (comparison) tools.

- Customisable 'skins' or settings (lets you choose your colours and layout so the environment best suits your preferences and needs, for example having the background in a choice of different colours for ease of reading).

- Cross-platform capability (if you work on multiple platforms you don't want to have to use different editors on each so having an editor that works on different platforms is a must for you).

- Multiple files can be opened at the same time (great for searching for keywords across multiple files, comparison of file contents and copying/pasting).

- File map (a small pictorial representation of your file so you can see where you are and move easily without having to scroll up and down all the time).

Some text editors to consider include:

- Sublime text (Windows, Mac, Linux): https://www.sublimetext.com/

- Visual studio code (Windows, Mac, Linux): https://code.visualstudio.com/

- Atom (Windows, Mac, Linux): https://atom.io/

- Notepad++ (Windows): https://notepad-plus-plus.org/

- Vim (Unix, Linux, Windows, Mac, iOS, Android, AmigaOS, MorphOS): https://www.vim.org/

- Brackets (Windows, Mac, Linux, Debian): http://brackets.io/

Test runners
These let you execute tests against your code. They may be scripting tools that let you automate execution, or they may be test applications that allow you to build and run tests of different types.

Some test-related tools to consider include:

- Cucumber: https://cucumber.io/

- JS-Test-driver: https://code.google.com/archive/p/js-test-driver/

- Selenium: https://selenium.dev/

111

- Load Runner: https://www.microfocus.com/en-us/products/loadrunner-load-testing/overview
- Rational Functional Tester: https://www.ibm.com/uk-en/marketplace/rational-functional-tester
- Jest: https://jestjs.io/
- Zephyr: https://www.getzephyr.com/
- QTP/UFT (previously Quick Test Professional by HP, now known as Unified Functional Testing): https://www.microfocus.com/en-us/products/uft-one/overview
- Telerik test studio: https://www.telerik.com/teststudio

You may work in an environment that uses **capture/replay tools**; these record a set of actions and then let you play them back. This is helpful in testing so that you can ensure you run the same sequence of actions every time, which is important when you retest the code to make sure an error is fixed.

Load test tools may be used to run load or stress testing, for instance to simulate a large number of people all trying to do the same action in your application at the same time.

Penetration test tools will run various tests that try to compromise the security of your code.

Any or all of these test tools may be needed to ensure good coverage of tests and thorough testing of the system before it moves to the next stage in the product life cycle. Some of the above are referred to as CAST tools (computer aided software testing).

FTP
FTP (File Transfer Protocol) client tools let you send files from your development machine to a server. This type of tool might be needed for website development, although some IDEs have this type of tool built in.

Some FTP tools to consider include:

- FileZilla: https://filezilla-project.org/

- CuteFTP: https://www.globalscape.com/cuteftp

- Secure FTP: https://secure-ftp.en.softonic.
com/?ex=DSK-1710.2

Developer tools in browsers

All modern browsers have built-in developer tools. These allow you to examine the website you are viewing, looking at the HTML, CSS and JavaScript and in many cases, editing it in the browser (note the in-browser changes are NOT saved to the file, they just let you see what effect the edit would have on the page). These developer tools also give single step debugging capability and let you see what the page would look like on different platforms, for example on mobile or tablet screens. Many browsers also have plug-ins that let you add extra functionality to the debugger, for example debugging a particular library – look up React Dev Tools in Chrome as an example.

IDE

Instead of using a plain text editor, some developers prefer (or their language choice requires them to use) an IDE. These tools allow you to type in code in the same way as text editors, but they also provide a whole host of extras. In some cases they have built-in debuggers, compile, packaging, deployment and run capabilities; in others they have that plus they add code into your projects in the form of libraries, or add structural support with built-in objects and capabilities. Some programming languages have specific IDEs that you need to use, for example Microsoft Visual Studio for developing any .Net language such as C#, VB.Net or ASP.Net.

Some IDEs to consider:

- Microsoft Visual Studio: https://visualstudio.microsoft.
com/

- Android Studio: https://developer.android.com/studio

- XCode: https://developer.apple.com/xcode/

- Eclipse: https://www.eclipse.org/ide/
- Oracle SQL Developer: https://www.oracle.com/uk/database/technologies/appdev/sql-developer.html

Boilerplates, templates or skeletons, and snippets

The concept of a **boilerplate** is a downloadable, copy-able or clone-able set of files which gives you a standardised starting point for a particular application or program type. These are readily available for web-based products[1] and provide an easy way to start out with code and tool setup, along with what should be a well-structured code template. The use of boilerplates in other non-web-based industries varies; they are more common in fairly modern areas such as mobile development and AI than in more traditional development sectors such as application software.

> Note that I am talking about the open source type of boilerplate; developers in all industries and sectors have been building and using their own boilerplates since programming began.

If you are going to look for a boilerplate (or if you are intending to build your own) here are some key things you should look out for:

- **Standards** – does it meet the standards you use at your company or in your team, for example naming standards or structural standards?

- **Documentation** – does it have documentation either built in to the code base or as a separate ReadMe file or document?

- **Scalability** – is it written for a particular platform or in such a way as to make it more efficient for certain sized products?

- **Use of third-party libraries** – is it reliant on third-party tools or libraries? If it is you should make sure the use of those libraries falls within the licences you want to use the product under, for example software for commercial use.

A **template** (also known as a skeleton) is a much simpler thing. Where a boilerplate offers a complete scaffold and tooling, a template is one or more lines of code that you use to start off your development.

A **snippet** is a few lines of code, similar to a template, but giving a subset of the code needed to develop a program. For example in a text editor, you might have templates and snippets available; a snippet could give you a simple class structure for a piece of code written in C#, while a template could give you a large amount of code that gives you a structure for a complete C# program (that may contain many classes, potentially created with many snippets).

Configuration management

A configuration management application is used throughout the life cycle of a product. It is used to keep track of everything to do with the product including design, requirements, setup, changes, testing, documentation and so on. It allows you to maintain information about the product which gives you quality control and consistency, as well as making it easy to see exactly what the current state of the product is.

Version/change control

Version/change control tools can be used separately but are generally used as part of a greater configuration management suite. They let you track and manage (approve or reject) the changes that are requested, in progress and completed on a product or project.

A widely used example of version control software is Git (https://git-scm.com/). Along with other products in this category it gives you a central repository so that you can keep the latest version of your code in one place. When people in a team want to work on the code they generally 'check out' a piece of code; the change control software keeps track of who is currently working on any piece of code at a given time. Once the code is 'checked in' again the software gives it a new version number so that all team members can be sure they are working on the latest version of the code.

Here are a couple of interesting articles on Git:

https://dev.to/taeluralexis/break-git-down-how-to-create-a-branch-from-master-and-make-your-first-commit-2960

https://code.likeagirl.io/git-what-422ca97e871

Both configuration management and change control software help to ensure that complex systems being worked on by teams of developers (and other team members) are kept stable, synchronised and up to date.

DEVOPS

DevOps is a fairly recent addition to the list of roles in IT. It is a combination of the names Development and Operations (or Developer and Operator) which were previously separate roles. The operator role originates from the big mainframe computers of the 1960s and 1970s when people were specifically employed to operate the machines. Over the years the need for this role changed; in many instances the role was being covered by infrastructure specialists or administrators. With the emphasis in modern development on agility, smaller teams and more virtualised, distributed systems and networks it was inevitable that more changes to this way of working occurred. The DevOps role emerged out of the need to have specialists to manage this new dynamic requirement.

116

One of the main benefits of DevOps (and a key reason behind its growing popularity) is that it helps you to ensure consistency across a product infrastructure; that is, consistency of setup, delivery, monitoring, environment, services and management. This is largely achieved now by means of automation; the infrastructure is code and it manages everything your (physical or virtual or both) system could need. In order to keep up with these new needs and usages developers are needed that can write resilient code which will manage life in the cloud with its potential network strains and outages.

If you would like to find out more and prove your knowledge about DevOps, BCS has a qualification: https://certifications.bcs.org/category/19356

DevOps-related products to consider:

- Puppet – automates infrastructure and application workflows (workflow is the name given to a series of tasks used to achieve an activity, for example the steps you take to send out email marketing material): https://puppet.com

- Git – mentioned earlier in this chapter, Git is a version control application: https://git-scm.com/

- Docker – lets you package up an application along with its dependencies, such as libraries, and deploy it as needed: https://www.docker.com/

- Vagrant – lets you build and manage virtual machine environments, useful if perhaps you are developing on a system that is not the same as the system the application is to be deployed on: https://www.vagrantup.com/

- Chef – software that allows you to package and deploy applications across multiple environments: https://www.chef.io/

UX/UI DESIGN AND PROTOTYPING

For UX (user experience) specialists (who help to ensure that the front-end design of a product is the best it can be for its users), one of the tools used to ensure a good user interface and experience is prototyping. Prototyping can be defined as building a physical working model of the proposed area within a system. Prototypes are then used to identify any possible flaws or problems with the proposed system by getting feedback from users, stakeholders, business analysts or other interested parties. You may be required to use prototyping as a developer.

There are two major approaches to prototyping: the Rapid (or throw-away) prototype and the Evolutionary prototype. With Rapid prototyping the main aim is to validate or define the system requirements. With Evolutionary prototyping the main aim is to deliver a working system to the users (usually quickly and with user involvement – this technique is commonly used with Agile). The two types of prototype can be further sub-divided as follows:

- Rapid:

  - Experimental – a prototype that is created to try out a technical difficulty.

  - Specific – a prototype that is created based on the requirements specification, to test whether the right assumptions and needs have been identified.

- Evolutionary:

  - 'True' Evolutionary – a prototype is created alongside the analysis and design. The initial design proposals are put forward in the form of a physical working model. The analysts, working with the users, gradually improve and develop this prototype until it meets a level of acceptability decided on by the user. When this happens, the prototype becomes the new system (Crinnion, 1992).

There are many different tools and techniques that can be used to build prototypes. Sometimes the most appropriate way to build a prototype is by using a combination of different tools (using the most appropriate one for each system component). The disadvantage to this is that you must also have a method of combining all the separately built components if you intend to use the prototype as part of the finished product.

There is an excellent set of resources at https://govuk-prototype-kit.herokuapp.com/docs that provide tutorials as well as examples on prototyping.

Building prototypes may involve the use of CASE tools (computer aided software engineering). These are applications that cover all aspects of a SDLC; for prototyping purposes the ones that allow you to design and, in some cases, generate the code for programs are primarily of interest. They are generally grouped into three categories: Upper Case tools (used in planning, analysis and design stages of a SDLC), Lower Case tools (used in implementation, testing and maintenance) and Integrated Case tools (which can cover all the stages of a SDLC).

An example set of CASE tools is this one by IBM: IBM Rational Rhapsody Designer: https://www.ibm.com/uk-en/marketplace/model-based-systems-engineering-platform

THE CONTINUOUS PRACTICES: INTEGRATION, DELIVERY AND DEPLOYMENT

The continuous practices are one way of applying quality control and improvement techniques in a development environment. They advocate small pieces of effort, applied frequently. They require developers to submit their work to a shared repository at least once a day (preferably more often); that code is then built using an automated script which may compile the code if necessary and run tests against it. They aim to reduce the time taken to deliver software by replacing the traditional practice of applying quality control after completing the development (as seen in the Waterfall SDLC earlier in this book). These processes fit well with Agile techniques and Scrum.

The key reason for adopting the continuous processes is to reduce the risks inherent in software development. They achieve this because:

- software is regularly integrated – helps to avoid the situation where you don't know if the latest piece of code works with existing code;

- software is regularly deployed – this ensures it works on the platform it is intended for;

- defects are detected and fixed sooner while they are still 'fresh in the mind';

- the current state of the system is easier to measure (and possibly demonstrate) – you know you always have a central source which contains the latest, working software;

- project visibility is improved for everyone involved in the production of code – you can see recent build status and quality metrics, and trends are easier to identify;

- you get feedback from the build every time you add new code to the central repository.

There are three different processes to continuous practices. The first is continuous integration, you always start with that and many companies stop there as it meets the needs of their development and gives them sufficient benefits without the need to adopt the other practices.

Continuous integration

Continuous integration (CI) essentially provides a pipeline which takes the code from the developer's desk to the next stage in the life cycle; this might be a test stage system but is not the live system. The developer writes their code and when ready will run a build script locally (which may compile the code and run tests against it). If this passes with no errors the developer will commit the code to a shared repository. If the company is using CI it is likely that it will be using some form of CI server or service (for example Hudson, Jenkins or CruiseControl) which will recognise that changes have been committed and will trigger the execution of an automated build script. This runs compilation and tests against the code (and maybe test installations) and gives feedback on the results. If there are errors, the code is withdrawn from the shared repository and the developer works to debug and fix it before resubmitting. Figure 5.1 illustrates this process.

Martin Fowler has an excellent article on CI: https://martinfowler.com/articles/continuousIntegration.html

Continuous delivery

Continuous delivery is the second process and does all that CI does as well as moving the code further along the pipeline (for example by running more tests or adding a trial deployment) by moving to a stage where it could be deployed to the live server (but isn't yet).

Continuous deployment

The final stage in the continuous processes is continuous deployment (shown in Figure 5.2), which takes code straight from the developer's desk through the product pipeline right out to the live environment.

Figure 5.1 Continuous integration

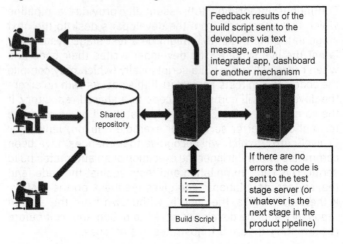

Feedback results of the build script sent to the developers via text message, email, integrated app, dashboard or another mechanism

Shared repository

Build Script

If there are no errors the code is sent to the test stage server (or whatever is the next stage in the product pipeline)

Figure 5.2 Continuous deployment

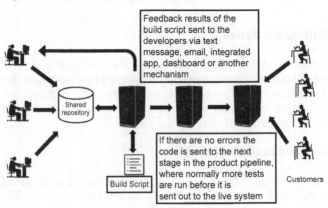

Feedback results of the build script sent to the developers via text message, email, integrated app, dashboard or another mechanism

Shared repository

Build Script

If there are no errors the code is sent to the next stage in the product pipeline, where normally more tests are run before it is sent out to the live system

Customers

The difference between continuous delivery and deployment is a business decision; you may choose not to go live because you may want to charge for the product, or because you may want to release a group of features together, or because the product itself does not work as staged delivery.

TEST DRIVEN DEVELOPMENT (TDD)

Traditional development methods used a technique where the code was written first, then tests were run against the code (see the Waterfall SDLC discussion in Chapter 2). Test driven development (TDD) turns that technique on its head. It creates a test first then builds code to exercise that test; you then refactor the test and refactor the code to run against it and so on.

The benefits of this technique are that at the end of the development you have a complete set of unit tests along with the code; you have also built your product using the minimum amount of code needed.

TDD will use whatever development language you use plus whatever language you use for test scripting; for example if you use HTML, CSS, JavaScript and React, you could write the code in JavaScript and the tests in Jest or Enzyme (Jest and Enzyme are both testing frameworks for JavaScript, they let you write tests that will test your JavaScript code).

There is a nice example walkthrough of a TDD session here, it is done in Java: https://technologyconversations. com/2013/12/20/test-driven-development-tdd-example-walkthrough/

Another excellent resource covers TDD and lists some tools to help you do TDD: http://agiledata.org/essays/tdd.html

BEHAVIOUR DRIVEN DEVELOPMENT (BDD)

Behaviour driven development (BDD) starts by looking at the required behaviour (requirements set by the business) of a system. It focuses on the functionality needed and is based around the concept of user acceptance testing. Devised by Dan North and often used in Agile, BDD looks at a product from the top down, looking at the context and overall functionality of the system being tested (as opposed to TDD which looks at the system from the bottom up, the single lines of code in the system being tested).

A variation on BDD is Specification by Example (SbE, also known as Acceptance test-driven development (A-TDD)) which is a collaborative technique used to define requirements and functional tests. It is based on the idea that people understand descriptions better if they are given an actual example rather than a descriptive concept.

One of the main features of SbE is that, when done well, it gives 'one source of truth' for the system; in other words the testing, requirements and business rules are all shown in one place.

See https://www.thoughtworks.com/insights/blog/specification-example and https://less.works/less/technical-excellence/specification-by-example.html, both of which have excellent articles about SbE and A-TDD.

In order to create and use BDD you will need suitable tools. Some popular tools are:

- Cucumber (Ruby-based): https://cucumber.io/

- JBehave (Java-based): https://jbehave.org/

- SpecFlow (.NET-based): https://specflow.org/

A key point about TDD and BDD is that in order to get good test coverage you need both techniques. Remember, TDD is a developer-centred, bottom-up technique, while BDD is a customer-centred, top-down technique.

SUMMARY

In this chapter we covered some of the tools and techniques that may be needed by developers. These could be applications used in the production of code or supporting tools used to manage that production throughout the software life cycle. We also looked at practices used by developers to enable them to do their job or to make it easier for them to do so.

The next chapter looks at career progression, suggestions for finding that all-important first role as a developer and possible options for where to go from there.

6 CAREER PROGRESSION FOR THE SOFTWARE DEVELOPER

Life is a series of building, testing, changing and iterating.
Lauren Mosenthal, Chief Technology Officer at
Glassbreakers

This chapter looks at securing (or changing) a developer role in the industry. It also considers a developer's career progression and how they may diversify into other areas and roles.

HOW DO YOU GET YOUR FIRST DEVELOPER ROLE?

Throughout this book there have been lists and descriptions of the skills and responsibilities required of a developer. Many of the things mentioned are relevant only in the context of the particular company, product and sector in which the developer works. It is not possible (unfortunately) to say that if you learn A, B and C you can get job X; the industry is too fast moving and the roles too varied to be able to do that with any degree of accuracy. What we will look at instead is possible routes into the role of software developer, the sort of thing you may expect in interviews, and ways that you could practise your skills while you look for that ideal role.

The other thing to remember is that there is no such thing as a typical path to employment as a developer; there will always be people who get into development in different ways from those described here. You may be one of those people. Don't be put off if you don't fit all the scenarios here; enthusiasm and drive plus a willingness to learn go a long way in the world of development.

These are some of the possible routes into a developer role (in no particular order). We will go through each one in turn, looking at the how and why of each:

- degree;
- apprenticeship;
- industry training;
- professional qualifications;
- self-teaching;
- from within an organisation.

Degree

There are many variations on computing degrees available; some will cover specialist topics such as AI or robotics, others are more generalist with a broad coverage of IT-related topics which may include analysis, design, development and testing. Look closely at the contents of prospective degrees if you have requirements for specific topics – universities are always happy to give you more information if you ask. The specific exam results needed to attend a course at university will vary depending on the course and the university in question; you can find this out ahead of time when you apply for a course. Some universities offer foundation courses or summer courses that can give you a taster, or an entry-level qualification as a base for further study.

A very large number of degree and postgraduate courses are available in the UK and worldwide. This short list of some of the universities and degrees provides a range of locations and topics to give you an illustration of the type of course you could attend:

- University of East Anglia – BEng Computer Systems Engineering: www2.uea.ac.uk/study/undergraduate/ degree/detail/beng-computer-systems-engineering

- University of Edinburgh – BSc in Artificial Intelligence: www.ed.ac.uk/studying/undergraduate/degrees/index. php?action=view&code=G700

- University of Stirling – BSc (Hons) Software Engineering: www.stir.ac.uk/courses/ug/natural-sciences/software-engineering/

- The University of Birmingham – BSc Computer Science: www.birmingham.ac.uk/undergraduate/courses/computer-science/computer-science.aspx

- University of Newcastle – School of Computing: www.ncl.ac.uk/computing/

- University of Oxford – Postgraduate courses list: www.cs.ox.ac.uk/softeng/handbook/awards.html

- Westminster – A selection of degree courses: www.westminster.ac.uk/computer-science-and-software-engineering-courses

- City University London – BSc (Hons) in Computer Science with Games Technology: www.city.ac.uk/study/courses/undergraduate/computer-science-with-games-technology

- Aberystwyth University – BSC in Computer Graphics, Vision and Games: https://courses.aber.ac.uk/undergraduate/computer-graphics-vision-games-degree/

As well as full-time degrees you have a choice of distance learning from well-known universities too:

- University of Oxford: https://www.conted.ox.ac.uk/about/advanced-diploma-in-data-and-systems-analysis

- Open University: www.open.ac.uk/courses/find/computing-and-it

- University of London: https://london.ac.uk/courses/computer-science

- University of Hertfordshire: https://www.herts.ac.uk/study/schools-of-study/computer-science/online-courses

- University of Liverpool: https://www.liverpool.ac.uk/computer-science/postgraduate/study-online/

Apprenticeship

An apprenticeship has many advantages as a way into any STEM (science, technology, engineering, mathematics) career. It is a real job, with hands-on practical experience, a salary and the chance to train while you work and the possibility of gaining further qualifications. You do not need to pay to attend a university course (in some cases the employer will pay for a course for you) so it may be appealing from a monetary point of view. The other advantage is that while other people are attending university you are earning money and getting that all-important experience.

The UK government has a website that includes some videos which detail various people's experiences of job seeking; some of these include people who have undertaken an apprenticeship in a STEM career. See https://mywayin.campaign.gov.uk/

The government also has an apprenticeships page: https://www.gov.uk/education/apprenticeships-traineeships-and-internships

Check the apprenticeship guide for vacancies and more information: www.apprenticeshipguide.co.uk/vacancies/

The IET has some excellent resources for apprentices and other job seekers: https://www.theiet.org/career/routes-to-engineering/apprenticeships/introducing-apprenticeships/find-an-apprenticeship/

Some colleges run combined apprenticeship and qualification courses. You may also find job fairs in your local area that spotlight apprenticeships and have employers available to give you more details about the sort of work you will be expected to do.

There are several levels of apprenticeship available; they differ based on qualification requirements.

An explanation of the qualification requirements (for England) are on the UCAS webpage: https://www.ucas.com/alternatives/apprenticeships/apprenticeships-england/entry-requirements-apprenticeships-england

UCAS also has a downloadable pdf that gives some good information about apprenticeships in general: https://www.ucas.com/file/120301/download?token=DPdwJ0EV

The employment 4 students website has a site dedicated to apprenticeships in IT: https://www.e4s.co.uk/jobs/5-it-apprenticeships.htm

Many large companies, the government and the armed forces take on apprentices every year. There is no upper age limit for apprenticeships, but you do have to be over 16 to apply.

Industry training or qualifications

When you are working on a particular development platform, for example Microsoft Windows, or using a particular technology, language or database you might find it helpful to get some form of qualification that validates your knowledge on that particular subject. Some employers will ask for these qualifications before you join a company while others will pay for you to take the qualifications after you have joined the company.

Many technology companies provide training and qualifications in their products; companies such as Microsoft and Oracle have a wide variety of certifications; these are recognised throughout the IT industry. In some companies you need to complete training at a recognised or certified provider before you sit the certification exams; for others you can self-study.

The advantage to these qualifications is that you are focusing on specific areas that may be of interest; the disadvantage is that you may have to retake qualifications when new versions of the product are released.

Examples of this sort of qualification at the time of writing include:

- MCPD – Microsoft Certified Professional Developer
- MCSD – Microsoft Certified Solution Developer
- Oracle Certified Associate
- Oracle Certified Professional, Java EE 5 Web Services Developer
- Oracle Certified Professional, Java ME 1 Mobile Application Developer
- AQA Level 3 Technical Level IT: Programming
- IBM Certified Associate Developer
- RHCJD: RedHat Certified JBoss Developer
- Cisco Network Programmability Developer Specialist

Many more qualifications are available; you should check the website of the company whose products you are interested in for full details and sometimes a list of accredited training providers is given.

As well as IT companies there are many independent training companies that can provide courses on a variety of topics. They may issue certificates or be able to arrange or advise on taking specific exams. It is always a good idea to speak to the training company to find out what the course covers, at what level and how the course is delivered, for example, whether it is distance learning, classroom-based or a bootcamp.

There are also qualifications available for topics related to development that may be relevant for the methodology or SDLC you use or the environment you work in. For example:

- Free short course on communications skills and teamwork: https://www.futurelearn.com/courses/categories/business-and-management-courses/communication-skills

- Microsoft has a downloadable ebook on their cloud-based database, Azure: https://azure.microsoft.com/en-us/resources/microsoft-azure-options-for-sql-server-relational-databases/

- Scrum qualifications for Scrum Master, Product Owner, Dev Team member and Nexus (Scrum for enterprise organisations): https://www.scrum.org/

- PRINCE2 Agile: https://www.axelos.com/certifications/prince2-agile

- Security for applications: https://www.globalknowledge.com/en-GB/Courses/Micro_Focus/Operating_Systems/FT2V0074

- Half-hour video introduction to SDLCs, available free from Udemy: https://www.udemy.com/sdlc-models/

Professional recognition and qualifications

This type of qualification is different from industry training or qualifications in that these qualifications do not just cover one technology or platform. These qualifications also tend to have a much broader scope of topics than the industry-specific ones; they often cover a range of skills and technologies needed to work in your chosen field. They are managed by professional bodies such as BCS[1] or the Institution of Engineering and Technology (IET);[2] they make membership, mentoring, continuing professional development (CPD) and qualifications available at various levels in line with industry requirements and standards.

The advantage to this route is that you could self-study, learning while doing another job, or you could get recognition for experience that you do not get via other formal qualifications. You also usually get membership of a professionally recognised group with all the support and advantages that that gives you.

Other associations, societies and institutes are available, but they may not all offer qualifications. Lists of these are currently available on the following sites:

www.directoryoftheprofessions.co.uk/sites-professions-IT-comp.html

https://en.wikipedia.org/wiki/List_of_professional_associations_in_the_United_Kingdom

Worshipful Company of Information Technologists: https://www.wcit.org.uk

BCS has degree-level qualifications that will prepare you for a career in IT. For full details see the website: https://www.bcs.org/get-qualified/international-higher-education-qualifications-heq/

Self-teaching

A 2019 report from hired.com[3] shows that one in five developers are self-taught, so this is by no means an unusual route into development work, although it does tend to be more common in areas such as web and mobile app development.

The first stage to this is to learn the language of your choice. Many routes are available to do this; the internet is a great resource with video-based sites giving something akin to a remote classroom experience, plus e-learning courses and community forums providing the mainstay of self-directed learning. Each language or technology will often have a website that provides tutorials on how to get started and how to use the language or technology for development.

You can attend trainer-led courses at IT training companies or further education (FE) centres, the difference being that the training companies tend to be shorter courses over contiguous days and are often more industry focused. The FE courses tend to be spread out over several weeks (or even months or years) but do give you plenty of time to practise what you learn before you move on to the next topic.

Another alternative to classroom-based learning is the 'bootcamp' – this is typically one or two weeks of intensive training and practical work coupled with (a lot) of self-guided reading and practice.

Working from books is also an option, your local library may order books for you to borrow depending on budgets and topics required (computer books can be expensive so it is often cheaper to get the books electronically if you have to buy them yourself).

Other sources of learning could include meetups (see https://www.meetup.com/) where you can meet people with similar interests in a friendly atmosphere. Some of the most popular ones relating to development include:

- Agile
- Building mobile apps
- Building webpages
- Coding clubs
- DevOps
- Girls/Women code
- Raspberry Pi
- And many that relate to specific languages, for example PHP

Note that these meetups are specific to geographical areas, and that while some areas may have a choice of meetups that you can attend, others may have none (that's a great opportunity for you to start a meetup for your area).

You might also like to try hackathons where people of different abilities meet (over anything from a few hours to a few days) to create software, webpages or apps that often benefit a good cause. Some, but not all of these, are done as competitions with prizes ranging from 'industry recognition' (in other words 'no money') to sponsorship or a chance to present your work to a large company.

Look for places where you can get a mentor, for example, BCS has a page devoted to just that: https://www.bcs.org/membership/member-communities/entrepreneurs-specialist-group/mentoring-programme/. You could also ask people if they would mentor you (be prepared for them to ask what exactly you want from that and also recognise that not everyone can be a mentor). Online mentoring sites are also available, try https://codingcoach.io/

People learn in different ways so it is important to understand what works best for you. If you are not sure, it is worth spending some time trying several of the methods outlined in this section until you find the way that works for you. The modern term for this is 'blended learning'.

In addition to learning a programming language you should also look for learning resources that show you how to apply the language correctly.

Here are a few useful sites to get you started:

- https://en.wikiversity.org/wiki/Introduction_to_Computer_Science
- https://www.codewars.com/
- https://ocw.mit.edu/courses/find-by-topic/#cat=engineering&subcat=computerscience
- https://learntocodewith.me/posts/code-for-free/

The next phase for self-teaching is practice. This is often done as you go along but you should also carry on doing this after learning the language. The best way to really understand how a language works and how it can be applied in the real world is to create things with that language. In addition to this it is beneficial to have a portfolio of work to show to prospective employers.

So, how do you get experience without having an actual job? Here is a selection of ideas you might like to try:

- Volunteer for a charity. Many voluntary organisations would be only too happy to have someone help with online work, whether it is maintaining or developing a website or looking after the applications they use. Who knows, if you do a good job they may provide a reference.

- Take part in code challenges or hackathons. Join in the coding community, join a team (or start a team), you will learn new things and the networking side may provide opportunities in future.

- Teach other people. No matter how little you feel you know, there will always be someone who would benefit from your help. Offer to help at a charity, school, meetup or online community such as Stack Overflow. Look at sites that interest you, see if they have opportunities for you to help, for example https://www.codefirstgirls.org.uk/become-an-instructor.html.

- Take up an internship, just be selective over who you ask and where you go.

- Create your own app, website or system, perhaps related to one of your interests or hobbies, or to help a family member or friend with one of theirs.

- Work on an open source project. Many developers collaborate to create work that is available publicly without cost or licence restrictions (or very light licence restrictions). Look for links on the websites of products you use or you like to see if you can help. Some large organisations that work on open source products or standards such as the World Wide Web Consortium (https://www.w3.org/) have working groups for some of those technologies; you could volunteer to be on a working group.

- If you already have a job, see if there are any opportunities at your place of work where you could employ your new skills.

- Look at other people's code. You can view source code on webpages and get open source code from sites such as GitHub. Find a product or site that you like and see if you can build your own version of it. (Don't just copy and paste the code though!)

- Attend conferences or seminars. While some of these do have a hefty price tag you should always look to see if there are any free tickets (for example for early signup) or discounted tickets that you may be able to get.

- Practise, whenever you can, wherever you can. If you don't practise writing the language you have learned you will soon forget it. Use it or lose it.

Moving to development from within an organisation

Many of the developers I meet have moved into software development from within the organisation where they worked in another role.

Generally, they had the type of role that either used a small amount of the skills used by developers or they worked closely with existing developers. Either way, they seem to have found an interest in software development and started to ask questions or do small bits of work either with the existing developers or independently.

One of the attributes all these people have in common is persistence. They kept asking questions (some people will be more helpful with answering than others), they kept practising and they asked within the company about possible moves to the technical role.

If you find yourself in this position consider the skills you have and the skills you need to gain, and how you can bridge the gap. Consider self-teaching, evening study or volunteering. If a move to development is not possible in your existing company then start to look at the sorts of jobs you would like to apply for in future and work towards gaining the skills necessary.

INTERVIEWS

It is not the intention of this book to give you advice on writing a CV; there are many resources available to help you do that. This section looks at some of the types of interview you may find yourself facing when you are looking for a developer role.

Let's first look at how you go about getting an interview.

Getting an interview

There are two common routes to getting an interview: applying for a job through an employment agency or approaching an employer directly. However, do not dismiss the power of networking or the possibility of getting a permanent role through voluntary work or internships (don't stay so long working for free that you feel you are being taken advantage of though).

Look at the websites of companies you would be interested in working for, see if they have a careers section that you can read. Be aware that some companies do not allow a direct approach and equally some companies only allow a direct application; it's up to you to find out which is which.

It would be impractical here to list all the possible employment agencies that you could use; look for ones that have jobs similar to the ones you are interested in; go in and talk to them to get a feel for the people who work there and be prepared to call them frequently to check up on progress for any applications they make on your behalf.

Interview types

The types of interview in this section are by no means an exhaustive list but the most common types of interview scenario.

Telephone interviews

Telephone interviews can be just verbal over the phone or via a video app such as Skype or GoToMeeting. They are often used as a way to screen candidates before a further interview at a later date or time.

A few tips specifically for telephone interviews include:

- Make sure you are prompt (call when you are supposed to or join the meeting with a minute or so to spare so you can key in any codes that are required to join).

- Ensure you have appropriate technology for the call, for example you may be required to download and set up Skype or similar software.

- Make sure you have a suitably quiet room or space to make the call where you won't be disturbed.

- Make sure you have a seat, you don't want to make the call while you are standing (or worse still, pacing up and down).

- If the call is over video link, for example using Skype, make sure you are dressed smartly and the area you are in is clear and presentable.

When I have had to download an unfamiliar app for this type of occasion I have done a quick test call to my own mobile first to make sure it works and I know how to use the application before the actual interview.

Questions and answers

This is a common interview technique. The interviewers (there could be one or more of them) ask you questions and expect the answers you give to be correct, with information that is up to date and relevant to the topic under discussion. You may be quizzed by subject matter experts or the question may be pre-prepared and just handed to the interviewer.

The questions are most commonly done via a face-to-face interview but could also be done via a telephone or video call.

The questions may revolve around a particular programming language, how you use it or the concepts it uses, for example classes or databases. You are also bound to get questions about yourself and your working practices and background experience.

A few tips specifically for question and answer style interviews are:

- Always prepare some questions to ask the interviewer as well (if you are given a chance to ask questions). Look up the company on the internet and ask relevant questions about what they do or about their development practices: for example, do they use pair programming?

- Read the job requirements carefully, you are most likely to be asked questions about specific key technologies or responsibilities. I like to create a tag cloud of the job specification, that highlights the words that are used most often and gives me a starting point for my preparation (try the TagCrowd site to create a tag cloud: https://tagcrowd.com/).

- Ask for clarification if you are unsure what you are being asked in one of these interviews (it is important to answer the question they are asking, not the one you think they are asking).

I have always found it better to admit that I did not know the answer if that is the case rather than trying to bluff. In some cases, I have asked what the answer is if I did not know it; even if you don't get that job at least you have learned something for the next interview.

Presentations

As the name suggests, this type of interview gets you to make a (normally stand-up) presentation. You may be presenting to one or more people in either a formal (training style room) or informal (meeting) room.

Getting you to do a presentation gives the prospective employer a chance to assess not only your technical skills (depending on what topic they ask you to present) but also your communication skills and your ability to time, organise and pre-prepare work. They may also be interested in your ability to present topics in an interesting and attention-grabbing way using text, graphics and presentation tools.

Some presentation-specific interview tips are:

- If they do not have a specific presentation tool that you need to use, why not use your developer skills to do something different, such as using JavaScript, HTML and CSS to create a presentation? (see Bostian, 2018)

- You will usually be given a time limit for the presentation; make sure you practise the presentation to check your timings.

- You may also be given a topic area or group of areas to choose from. Pick one that you are (most) confident on, preferably a topic that relates to the job requirements.

- Do not try to fit too much onto a slide, about six key points is a good maximum (with around six to eight words per point).

- Do not just read out what is on your slide, the slide is there to provide key words and graphics to support your narrative.

- You may have to send the presentation in advance. If this is the case ask what format they want the presentation in.

- Ask if they want you to bring handouts. Handouts can show that you are keen and able and may make your presentation stand out among a crowd.

- You should also ask if they have a laptop or computer there already or if you need to take your own laptop (if you have one) in order to give the presentation.

- Also ask what type of connectors (HDMI, VGA) they have if you are taking your own laptop so there are no surprises when you get there.

- After your presentation you will probably have some questions from the audience. Take the time to think through possible questions and answers beforehand.

- Interviewers would not be surprised if people are nervous; ask if you can have a glass of water before you start (sometimes it is handy to take a sip of the water to give yourself thinking time).

Occasionally you may be asked to do a presentation during the interview with little or no notice; this may be to assess your reaction to pressure. If this is the case, don't panic – pick a topic you are very familiar with, keep the presentation simple. The best way to avoid panic is to prepare thoroughly in advance. I like to have a small presentation prepared just in case.

Projects

Interview projects are where you are asked to build a small website, app or program. They could be take away (where you are given the task and asked to bring or send the result by a specific date) or in-house (where you build them on site during the interview), with or without internet connectivity. They are set to assess your analysis, creativity, problem-solving and technical skills (possibly under pressure).

Tips for project-based interviews are:

- Even if you do not get a chance to finish the project it is still worth commenting on the sections that are yet to be completed as it will show what you intended to do and give the prospective employer an idea about your thinking processes.

- Make sure you understand the brief and don't be afraid to ask questions. This shows you are thinking things through and that you can formulate relevant questions.

- If you are allowed to pick the language or format for the result, for example a webpage or app, pick the format that you are most familiar with; you do not have to use all the latest libraries and techniques unless you are specifically asked to do so.

- Spend some time planning what you are going to do and how you are going to do it. This planning time is just as important as the development of the project and shows your working practices.

If I have the time on a project (that's usually if it is a take away project) I like to do some small amount of documentation too, both on my planning and if possible a little about how to use the app. This shows prospective employers that you can do planning and documentation as well as development.

Tests

These can be technical online or written tests or exams; they could be in the form of an essay, multiple choice questions or a mixture of both.

Tips for tests include:

- Make sure you read the instructions carefully before you start.

- Work out how much time you should allocate to each question.

- If you are stuck on a question (if possible) carry on to the next question and come back to the one you are stuck on at the end. It's better to miss one question than lose too much time and miss several questions later.

- Just like for any test (or exam), prepare your topic areas, do some reading or practice tests on the test topics beforehand.

Group or teamwork

Group or teamwork is a technique used when there are a large number of people being interviewed or where the employer has several vacancies to fill. You may be given a task or series of tasks to complete with other people; they may also be interview candidates or they could be existing employees. In general, the employer will be looking for teamwork skills (working with others not competing with them), organisational skills and problem solving, leadership and persuasiveness in addition to your enthusiasm, communication skills and ability to work (possibly) under pressure.

Tips for teamwork-based interviews are:

- When taking part in a group exercise make sure you contribute and follow the instructions you were given.

- Have faith in your views but do not become argumentative if you cannot persuade others in the group.

- Make sure you listen to other people's views and be prepared to follow them if they make sense in the scenario.

One specialist type of teamwork is pair programming, mentioned in Chapter 3. Even if you have not done this before, you should take the time to find out about it so you know what to expect.

Personality tests or profiling

Some employers will ask you to do a psychometric or personality test. Be careful not to try to 'fool' these tests by answering what you think they want. These tests do not have a right or wrong answer; they are there to give the prospective employer an idea about you as a person, so be honest.

Two different types of test may be used: personality tests, which help to assess your interests, values and motivations, and aptitude tests, which help to assess your reasoning or cognitive ability.

Here are a couple of example tests for you to try:

https://www.assessmentday.co.uk/personality-questionnaire.htm

https://www.16personalities.com/

General interview tips

An ex-colleague of mine familiar with conducting interviews mentioned to me that he has been horrified by how ill-prepared some of the candidates he has interviewed were.

His principle is that you should prepare for an interview as if it was a first date – if you don't make a good impression you will never see them again.

Some of his key tips are:

- Know what job you are applying for. (Yes, he interviewed someone who did not know what they had put on their application form. No, they didn't get the job they didn't know about.)
- Don't put anything on your CV that you can't actually talk about.
- Only put things on your CV that are relevant to the job you are applying for. In general, you may want to have several 'versions' of your CV.
- If you have paperwork to give to someone, then hand it to them (don't throw it across the table). Find out what paperwork is needed before you go and have it filled in ready.

CONTINUING PROFESSIONAL DEVELOPMENT (CPD) FOR DEVELOPERS

Ongoing professional and personal skills development is essential for any developer; without it they will be quickly out of date in the fast-moving technology sector. So CPD is not only good practice, it is a way to keep track (and prove) your ongoing learning and skills improvement in your role. Some companies make it part of your employment contract that you must keep and obtain a certain number of CPD 'points' or hours in a year; indeed, in some companies your yearly assessment depends in part on your CPD.

CPD can be tracked by keeping records of what you do and when. The sorts of things you can track for CPD include:

- Certifications: any exams you pass or tests you take, whether they are generic (for example Agile/Scrum) or product-specific (for example Oracle).

- Courses: what course, what contents, course duration and when the course was taken. Keep any certificates that are issued for the course (even if it is just a certificate of completion or attendance).

- Projects: both work-based projects and any (development-related) work you do at home, for example if you help to maintain a school or club website.

- Conferences: helpful to note any lectures or workshops you attend at the many developer conferences that are available every year. These can be generic conferences or language-specific ones.

- Events: company events such as product launches or customer events (if you get invited to these).

- Seminars attended, talks or lectures: either formal or informal, for example at a meetup event.

- Self-taught courses or videos: whether paid for or free offerings.

- Voluntary work: including information about what organisation you volunteered with, what you did and possibly who supervised your work, if applicable.

The IET has good website content on CPD. It is aimed at IET members but generally applicable to anyone who is interested in CPD: https://www.theiet.org/career/professional-development/continuing-professional-development/what-is-cpd/

A UK-based website specifically aimed at explaining and promoting CPD: https://cpduk.co.uk/explained

MOVING UP THE LADDER: WHERE NEXT FOR DEVELOPERS?

The SFIA skills levels (shown cross-referenced against BCS certification and experience levels in Figure 6.1) for software developers provide a good guideline as to the sorts of skills and experience you need to further your role as a software developer within the industry. The final section of this chapter looks at possible pathways for career development.

As always there is no 'standardised' way to progress as a developer, although it is important to understand what career paths are available within your existing company or organisation.

In general, with increasing seniority the developer role starts to take on more responsibility, a broader range of skills and a greater participation in the system life cycle. This often means getting involved in the pre-project stages, advising on technical capabilities and choices in how the project is done. It may include team leading or management activities, mentoring, and standards and tool specification.

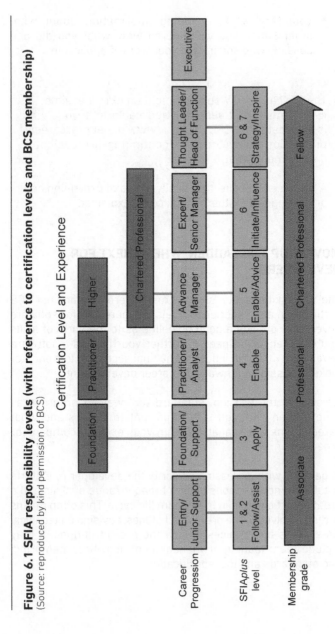

Figure 6.1 SFIA responsibility levels (with reference to certification levels and BCS membership)
(Source: reproduced by kind permission of BCS)

Certification Level and Experience

Career Progression	Entry/ Junior Support	Foundation	Practitioner	Higher		Thought Leader/ Head of Function	Executive
		Foundation/ Support	Practitioner/ Analyst	Advance Manager	Expert/ Senior Manager		
				Chartered Professional			
SFIA*plus* level	1 & 2 Follow/Assist	3 Apply	4 Enable	5 Enable/Advice	6 Initiate/Influence	6 & 7 Strategy/Inspire	
Membership grade	Associate		Professional	Chartered Professional		Fellow	

If further progression is not possible within your organisation you may start to look at other companies or consider going freelance as a self-employed developer. There are some advantages to being freelance: you can choose the jobs you accept, you generally get a higher rate of pay and you manage your own time. There are also disadvantages as well. You have to look for the next contract all the time and if you are not working you are not earning (also no one pays your pension, sick pay or holiday pay when you are self-employed). You also have to pay for your own training or any certifications you need. You may consider working through an agency, which will generally have a broad range of contacts and will find the work for you, but it will take a percentage of your earnings for doing so.

> I have been self-employed for a long time and wouldn't have it any other way. However it's not a suitable lifestyle for everyone. If you are considering it you should look very carefully at the pros and cons with respect to your own circumstances and skill set.

Sometimes it is not possible to progress further within a company from a role as senior developer without moving into management. This is a difficult situation. If you don't fancy this, you may have to choose between staying where you are with no possibility of career progression and moving to another company with a broader spectrum of developer roles available. There is no simple answer to that dilemma, every person must weigh up the pros and cons and make their own choice.

SUMMARY

This chapter covered some possible routes into work as a software developer and highlighted the types of interview that a developer may face. It also looked at CPD and career progression for software developers.

The next, and final, chapter, gives you some case studies; true stories from people currently working as developers across a wide range of industries and sectors.

7 CASE STUDIES: DEVELOPERS IN THEIR OWN WORDS

I would love to change the world, but they won't give me the source code.

Anon

This chapter gives you some stories from developers in their own words. I didn't want to interview people and get them all to answer the same questions. Instead I wanted to show you how different developer roles, journeys to becoming a developer and experiences of developers are, and to show the diversity of people working in development.

The one common factor you should notice in these studies is the passion that all these people have for their roles, and how creative they find the work. Yes, the work can be frustrating and challenging at times (aren't all interesting roles?) but the sense of achievement you'll get far outweighs any problems you may encounter along the way.

You will notice that not all the people in this chapter have the title 'software developer'. One is a UX engineer and one is a web developer, for instance, but all the people in this chapter have one major thing in common: they all write code in order to develop products that run on computers. UX engineering and web development are specialisms of the software developer role in the same way as front-end development and full-stack development are specialisms (as described in Chapter 2).

You can only become truly accomplished at something you love. Don't make money your goal. Instead, pursue the things you love doing, and then do them so well that people can't take their eyes off you.
(Maya Angelou (1928–2014), an American poet, singer, memoirist and civil rights activist)

CASE STUDY 1: LEARNING A NEW PROGRAMMING LANGUAGE

In this first case study we look at the experience of Jeremy (Jez) who moved from an older legacy programming language (RPG) running on older (non-PC-based) hardware to learning and working with a new programming language (C#) on PCs. This story illustrates how you can move from one programming language and hardware platform to another during your career as a developer.

Jeremy Clarke – Developer

I have 25+ years' experience programming with an IBM procedural language (RPG). During this time, I had very little exposure to the Microsoft Windows environment or development on that platform. Nine months ago, I chose to move into something more modern. After researching the job market I chose to start with C#. Python was also a possibility for later exploration, but I felt one language at a time was enough.

My early learning experience came exclusively in the form of YouTube videos, where there is a wealth of free resource available and I wanted to make the early part of the process as cheap as possible. Searches for C# courses resulted in a couple of good leads (as well as many dead ends). Among the good ones were videos from the channels Programming with Mosh and IAmTimCorey.

It may have been my choice of courses, but I found my lack of experience in Windows held me up; most of the teachers assumed a certain degree of knowledge of the environment which I didn't have. However, any searches I did for guides or courses on the Windows environment (.Net) didn't yield the information I was looking for.

In an attempt to get a deeper knowledge of the .Net development environment I turned to Microsoft Virtual Academy (MVA). The site has a plethora of videos on Visual Studio and C# (and other topics of course, but I was only interested in these). On the whole, MVA courses are very good, they have a lot of depth and cover their topics well; however they take a lot of time.

After getting a new job as a C# developer I was lucky enough to gain access to a paid learning site – Pluralsight. I found Pluralsight very useful, it has a nice balance between instructions such as 'write this here' and explanations like 'this is why we're doing this'. I've followed along with several courses replicating the programs as I go and I've got a lot of useful experience out of it.

After all of the above, I have to say I still found writing my own code and making mistakes the most useful method of learning. Deciding on an application to write and diving in, then Googling issues as I go helped me learn far more than passively watching videos or trying to follow along.

Now I have a level of experience in C#, I'd like to attend an instructor-led intermediate course in the near future. I'm hoping to plug some of the gaps in my knowledge in this manner.

CASE STUDY 2: A DAY IN THE LIFE OF A UX ENGINEER

The work Emma does as a UX engineer is very varied and serves to illustrate 'a day in the life' of a developer. As well as working full-time, Emma works on open source projects, writes blogs and contributes to social media sites. Her case study also gives you some ideas about how teams work together in product development.

Emma Bostian – UX Engineer at LogMeIn and Founder of Coding Coach

Each morning around 6 a.m. I wake up, and if I have some extra time, I'll work on my open source project, Coding Coach, or complete a few smaller, personal tasks I've been putting off. I take the train to work around 7.55 each morning and arrive at the office around 9.

153

My day typically starts by grabbing a coffee with my colleague and talking about the tech industry. He was the first person who encouraged me to get back on Twitter to promote my blog posts, and ever since that moment I've been thoroughly enjoying technical community interactions.

Around 9.30, I get started on my tasks. I like to start with the larger, more thought-intensive tasks as I find I'm most productive in the morning. This usually involves developing React components or building our UI framework.

As a UX Engineer, my primary role is focused on building and maintaining a design system (design language, component library and style guide). We're still in the early phases of development so my current tasks involve developing an architecture for the component library and building out a new style guide to house all of our design and development assets. I've been developing this using React and Gatsby.

I only started using React about a year ago. Prior to React I was extremely invested in Vue.js, but when I switched companies from IBM to LogMeIn, I had to pick up React. I have really enjoyed learning and using React, Redux and TypeScript to build enterprise applications. And it was only within the last few months that I found a love for Gatsby: a static site generator for React. It makes creating fast, SEO-friendly websites extremely easy.

This is one reason I love being a UX engineer; there's more autonomy to choose your tech stack. In well-established engineering roles, you have to play to the tune of their tech stacks. When you get to make the stack decisions, the world is your oyster.

This not only involves coding but also researching proper accessibility for these elements. Often, when developing

154

custom elements, accessibility can suffer so part of my job is to ensure W3C accessibility compliance.[1]

Around 12 my team eats lunch. My lunchtime activities vary day-to-day but will consist of one of the following: taking a German course (since moving to Germany, I've been taking lessons), team lunch, 'Sketch-and-lunch'.

> Sketch-and-lunch is an activity my design team does to keep up to date with design skills and learn some new ones.
>
> I'm also in the process of creating a 'code-and-lunch', to teach my designer teammates how to code. It's important, especially as a UX engineer, to obtain both design and engineering skills. I love the collaboration between design and engineering.

Between 1 and 4 p.m. is typically 'heads down' working time. I generally don't have a lot of meetings during the day. If I do have a meeting, it's with one of the product development teams to discuss collaboration and sprint goals.

I commute home around 4 in the afternoon and arrive home around 5. Half of our design team sits in California so once a week from 6 to 8 p.m. we'll have a UX Sync and a Design System Standup.

In the evenings I either blog, work on Coding Coach, or develop content for Egghead.io, an online learning platform. I enjoy creating content around CSS, Sass, and animations for beginners in web development. I often find that I'm mentally exhausted by the end of the day and can't focus much more on coding, so I may end up just reading a book instead.

Before I know it, it's time to get up and get ready for work again!

CASE STUDY 3: THE ROAD TO BEING AN EXPERIENCED DEVELOPER

Chris's story describes his journey from hobby coder to developer. Chris talks about looking at all areas of development and taking courses with a broad topic range before narrowing down the specific area he wanted to work in. He also talks about using an industry placement to verify those choices.

Chris Ashton – Developer

I'd just had my A-level results and it wasn't looking good. I was hoping to get into medicine, which demanded top grades in the sciences, and I had narrowly missed out.

I took an unplanned year out to figure out what I wanted to do instead. During the day, I worked at a bank to earn money and to pass the time. At night, I did what I loved – building websites. These websites would never even see the light of day, but I spent hours tweaking CSS to perfect the experience of my imaginary users. I 'viewed source' on every website that I came across that looked new or interesting. I experimented with copying and pasting snippets of JavaScript, not understanding its contents but amazed by its effects.

I spent my gap year considering what to do next when I had my eureka moment: why not do what I love best and turn my coding hobby into a career?

I lacked the confidence in my technical abilities to turn it into a career immediately – sure, I'd managed to figure out how to build a calculator in PHP, but was it well written? Would it fall over in the real world?

Moreover, I was just starting out; did I know if I wanted to work on the web, or if I'd prefer to build software, or video games? After carefully reviewing all options, I enrolled on a Software Engineering course at Aberystwyth University, which seemed the most 'well rounded' of courses that could be applied to any programming career.

Though I absolutely loved my course and all the new areas of programming it exposed me to, I continued to find myself drawn mostly to web development. Between my second and third year of university I had the opportunity to do a 'sandwich year' in industry. I saw a position for a Trainee Web Developer at the BBC in central London, which looked perfect.

That 13-month placement was the beginning of an exciting and prosperous web career. Over the years I was able to rise through the ranks, working on some really fun and interesting projects along the way, using technologies such as ES6 JavaScript, SCSS, Handlebars, React, Node, Webpack and service workers. This culminated in leading the delivery of the new BBC article page in April 2019. I'm now looking at my next challenge and have accepted a development role in government. I can't wait!

CASE STUDY 4: HOW I BECAME A WEB DEVELOPER

This story from Eva shows how a career change into development and self-teaching can lead to new opportunities, not only in work, but in the wider development community, providing a helping hand to others in the same or similar positions.

Eva Dovc – Web Developer and Creator of GirlsCode MK

I've been a web developer for such a small proportion of my professional life that sometimes I find myself doing a double-take when someone refers to me as a programmer. Coding feels new, with vast oceans of unknowns (search engines and web dev. forums are my best friends), and I love it.

I started coding in 2017, and one of the best lessons I can pass on to those who are thinking about becoming web developers is that there are many paths to reach the same destination.

I'm self-taught. I used to work as an ecommerce executive, which mostly meant looking after online shops, from managing inventory to tweaking basic HTML to make listings look appealing. Some parts of my job were pretty dull and routine, and I wondered if there may be an app, a program of some kind that could do the menial bits of my job for me. Turns out what I needed was too specific, so there wasn't a one-size-fits-all solution. I took it as a challenge to find a way to crack that puzzle: to program a bit of code that could run searches for me. And I did it!

It felt really good. There it was: my very own automation.

Around that time, I heard about Django Girls, a series of workshops around the world that facilitate a welcoming space for women to learn how to code, with the ultimate aim to improve diversity in tech. Django Girls host one-off events that give you a taste of coding. The problem was that there weren't any events close to Milton Keynes, where I live. But there was one in Belfast...

I didn't know what to expect at first, but within the first hour, it was clear I had found a community I could belong to. That was a watershed moment that kick-started my career change, and I've heard from many other female developers that finding a welcoming, safe community of coders has been a vehicle to build their expertise and confidence.

I started learning online. I found Free Code Camp and other online tutorials, but I was missing having someone experienced who could help me out when I got stuck. So, with the support of my wife, I decided to quit my job and start a learning group in my own county that would rely on volunteer teachers to help other women who, like me, wanted to become web developers or software engineers, but who didn't consider that a full-time computer science degree was either possible or needed. Thus, GirlsCode MK was born, a free fortnightly workshop for women of all ages and backgrounds who want to learn how to code together.

I adapted my own learning to my family circumstances, which has worked well for me but hasn't been without its challenges.

I've learned from tutorials, from trial-and-error experiments, through books and by asking a lot of questions to the growing community of volunteer coaches that joined GirlsCode MK as mentors. I discovered that there are too many languages and technologies out there, and it can be intimidating – should I be learning only JavaScript? Is React the hot new thing? Should I stick to front-end or venture into back-end tech? Should I start applying for jobs or wait until I know more? How about a bootcamp, apprenticeship or some freelance work? But that happens to all of us.

Having mentors and friends who shared their pathways and knowledge with me helped me realise that coding is like facing new puzzles all the time and that while I can't have all the answers all the time, I don't need to have them. It's OK not to know.

In the past 18 months, GirlsCode MK grew its membership from the two founding members, my wife and me, to almost 500 members, organising more than 60 free events. Thanks to my work with GirlsCode MK, I was granted the 2018 MK Women Leaders award.

I now work full-time as an independent web developer. While I know that the learning journey is not over – and never will be – I'm excited to discover what comes next.

CASE STUDY 5: THE ENTERPRISE SOFTWARE DEVELOPER

Simon owns a company that specialises in developing applications for other businesses. As well as running a company he still does development work himself and is currently working as a freelance developer. Simon's story talks about the ups and downs of working as a developer, the challenges and opportunities, as well as describing why it's still the only career he would ever consider.

Simon Kemp – Freelance Developer, Owner of March-Web

In any job, there are good days and bad. Highs and lows. Days when you question why you do it. Days when it is very clear why you do it. For me, there are a number of good reasons why I'm a software developer. In fact, reasons why I *need* to do it!

Yes, the money is good. I'm now and have been for many years well paid – compared with many others of my age. But money doesn't buy everything and there needs to be more than a comfortable pay packet to justify getting up and going to work in the same industry for 40 years! The main reasons that I so enjoy being in the Information Technology (IT) business is that I love to create and build things. To see the happiness on the faces of my users when they see how much easier I've made their jobs. How much more they can now do without resorting to extra hours. How they can now do other things that they've not had the chance to get around to for months or even years. For example, a recent system I built saved someone a day a week of work. Now, instead of having to feed their very manual processes, they could spend more time thinking about what they can do to improve their supplier relationships, their departmental staff knowledge and the other inefficient things they do where they've never had the time to work out something better.

The challenges to me are many and varied – I've worked with businesses in industries as diverse as defence, leisure cruising, healthcare, pharmaceuticals, agriculture and power generation – and I always get excited when working to understand their processes, their needs, what they currently do and what they'd like to do better. Another example was the creation of a project management system that brought together worker timesheet data from many different sources at this large site with over 2,000 employees. The big challenge was to understand not just the total hours (and therefore cost) of the time spent working on all their projects as a whole, but the consolidated picture across all projects in progress – projects by group and individual projects themselves. It also involved identifying in a very clear and graphical way where the future pinch points were by department as the various projects competed with each other for valuable expert worker time. This was made more 'fun' by the fluid nature of the projects, meaning that they often didn't use the experts when they previously expected to – so re-planning was a constant challenge. The system I built allows them to do this in a way that they didn't even think possible. With the output of lots of planning spreadsheets with various colour- and word-coded departmental allocations, they were able to visualise the situation and make adjustments to get the best and most efficient future plan. All this for over 100 users! Clearly, there were many different benefits to be had by various users. Some were seen more as net contributors, while management had a desperate need for the big picture which wouldn't have been possible without the efforts of all.

Technology is a great enabler and its democratisation has seen everybody's lives change beyond recognition. However, it's not all roses, and IT is riddled with fashionistas, people who have to ride the newest wave and in some cases, people who need to create that wave – irrespective of whether it's in the right place or for the right reasons. I've seen many clever new IT fashions come and go and I'm sure I'll see many more. In fact, I used to subscribe to a PC magazine that confidently predicted a newly released piece of software would be the end of software development, as it had the ability to create an application on its own. However, I'm still doing this job 35 years later and the business that gave the world 'The Last One' is no more!

Working with other people's code can be challenging, I sometimes end up picking up the pieces at companies where the unaware business has had someone's personal research and development project sprawl its meandering way through the creation of a maze of (unnecessarily complicated, expensive and difficult to maintain) program code. Developers generally have a belief that they should be able to do what they want and in the way they see fit. This makes it so much more important to ensure they don't! While innovation can bring cost savings and much improved efficiency, the cost of writing off needless and unstructured or poorly designed applications more than outweighs any previous advantages. Care is always needed when looking to make use of the latest big thing. Because it usually isn't as helpful or useful as the supplier or evangelist wants, hopes or needs it to be.

One of my biggest bugbears is the constant need some manufacturers have to change things by way of 'enhancements' or 'improvements'. Particularly when they're happily forcing you to rewrite your application – mainly so they can sell another product – and, in some cases, get their teeth even further into your budgets.

The period to obtain valid return on investment (ROI) for some IT projects is notoriously short because of it. And this means that some businesses are very cautious when it comes to engaging with IT.

As a result, I have a combination of a conservative approach and innovation that makes use of tried and tested techniques that are well thought out and designed while embracing new skills purely on the basis of fitness for purpose. Risk mitigation or even avoidance can be more valuable than the embracing of the latest fashion and buzzwords.

Finally, every member of an IT department – however small or large – should be very clear that they are a member of a vitally important SERVICE department to the business. They are not the business itself.

CASE STUDY 6: THE GRADUATE'S JOURNEY

While Simon's story is from someone who has worked in the industry for a long time, this story from Zara describes the role from the point of view of someone just starting out in their career as a developer. Zara shows that even with a degree the best way to really learn development is by doing it and helping others with their development.

Zara Ahmed – Graduate (Technical) Developer at AVEVA

As a child, and for the majority of my life, I have perceived the world around me as an avid observer. This curiosity has always sparked the creative element inside me and therefore I like to subconsciously believe that this creativity is at the heart of my love for technology. I particularly enjoyed, and spent most of my time, reading and engaging in still-life drawing. This was until I discovered my first desktop computer at the age of nine. I was immediately fascinated by it and immersed myself in all the possible things that I could potentially do with it.

I carried this interest into secondary school, where I learnt the basics of developing a website. This curiosity eventually led to securing an offer to study computer science (CS) at Aston University. Although I was enrolled as a CS student, I was still apprehensive as to what career paths I would take and whether I would be able to survive, long-term, as a woman in technology.

I luckily stumbled across an internship during my first year at university. This gave me an opportunity to appreciate the nature of programming – the act of 'learning by doing'. My work involved researching indoor navigation, while learning how to develop apps on Android devices. Although challenging at first, this internship made me appreciate that any goal is achievable, and in turn changed my perspective for my future in tech.

My university years flew by very quickly, but I made sure that I went the extra mile to gain as much exposure to learning, programming and networking as I could before joining the world of work. I believe most of my passion and motivation behind wanting to become a developer are due to the supportive female networking events that I attended. They provided a safe haven, where I was able to discuss and overcome any difficulties I had. This eventually led to me providing support to others, as opposed to being on the receiving end. I was fortunate to be part of the Code First:

Girls organisation, where I led a course that taught women in university, from backgrounds other than tech, how to develop a website. In this particular scenario – I 'learned by teaching'.

After I completed my bachelor's, I managed to secure another internship, with Microsoft Research. Working with a tech giant felt very daunting at first, but the talent and support that surrounded me helped accomplish my goal of developing a chat bot and being part of a research paper, which was extremely rewarding.

Although I took the traditional route of going to university to learn the skills of becoming a developer, I feel that self-effort has also played a huge part. The different styles of learning have made me who I am today, whether that was learning by being taught at university, learning by doing in my internships or learning by teaching others the knowledge I have.

I have recently joined AVEVA as a Graduate (Technical), where I hope to learn more skills and improve my programming by working on the industrial software they have to offer.

SUMMARY

This chapter illustrated the sort of work done by software developers. It also showed the difference in developer roles and the different journeys people took to become developers.

In my experience the software developer role gives you the opportunity to constantly learn new things, whether they are new systems or platforms, new programming languages or new uses for those languages. It is one of the joys of the computing industry that it is always progressing, expanding and inventing new ideas, concepts and devices. It is an exciting and engaging industry to be in with lots of possibilities for imagination, creativity and to progress in your career.

APPENDIX:
TL;DR

Obviously I'd like you to read (and enjoy) the whole book but more importantly I'd like the book to be helpful to you. Sometimes you just need a quick summary of key points. With this in mind I've added this TL;DR (too long; didn't read) appendix. This chapter will use diagrams to summarise some of the key points from the book.

Figure A.1 Book road map

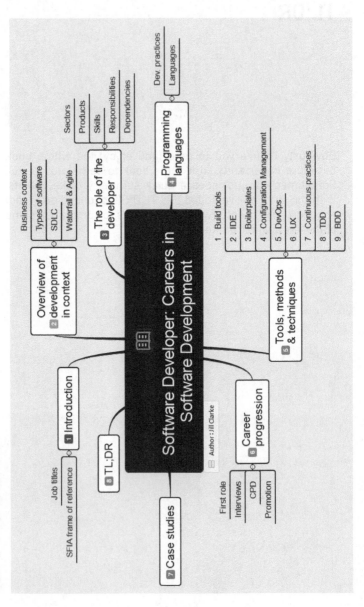

Figure A.2 Developer role from SFIA (Source: Central image by permission of SFIA)

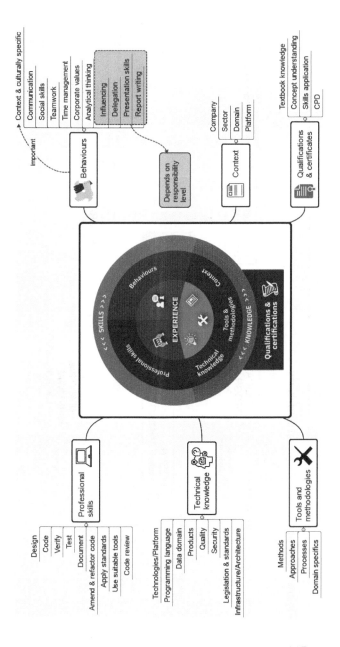

Behaviours
- Context & culturally specific
  - Communication
  - Social skills
  - Teamwork
  - Time management
  - Corporate values
  - Analytical thinking

Depends on responsibility level (Important)
- Influencing
- Delegation
- Presentation skills
- Report writing

Context
- Company
  - Sector
  - Domain
  - Platform

Qualifications & certificates
- Textbook knowledge
- Concept understanding
  - Skills application
  - CPD

Professional skills
- Design
  - Code
  - Verify
  - Test
  - Document
- Amend & refactor code
- Apply standards
- Use suitable tools
  - Code review

Technical knowledge
- Technologies/Platform
- Programming language
- Data domain
- Products
- Quality
- Security
- Legislation & standards
- Infrastructure/Architecture

Tools and methodologies
- Methods
- Approaches
- Processes
- Domain specifics

Figure A.3 Types of development summary

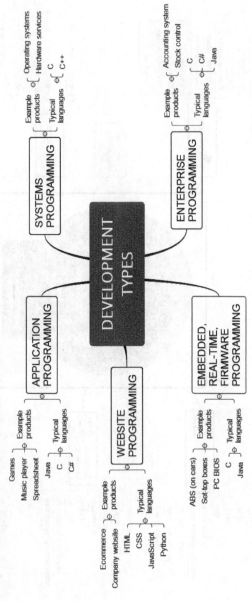

Figure A.4 Developer participation in Waterfall SDLC; typically in the build and support stages

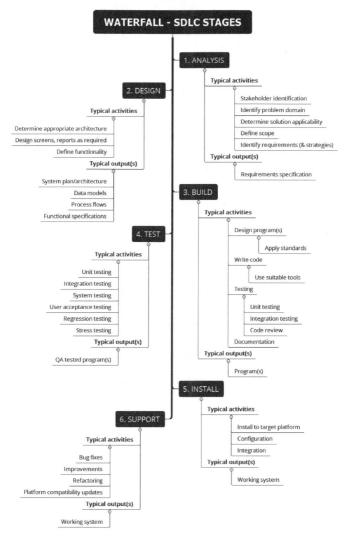

Figure A.5 Developer participation in Agile/Scrum; typically as part of the development team (Source: Original diagram with no changes made. Reproduced by kind permission of Neon Rain Interactive (https://www.neonrain.com/agile-scrum-web-development/). Licence: https://creativecommons.org/licenses/by-nd/3.0/nz/)

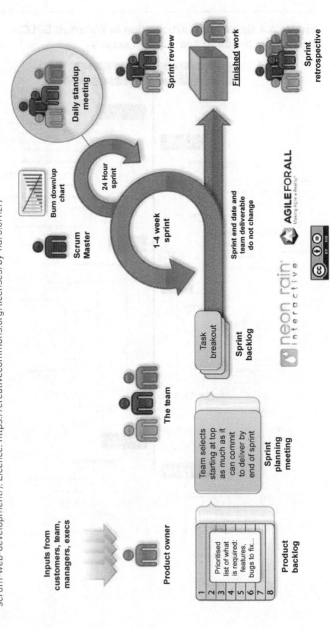

Figure A.6 Developers' key knowledge and skills

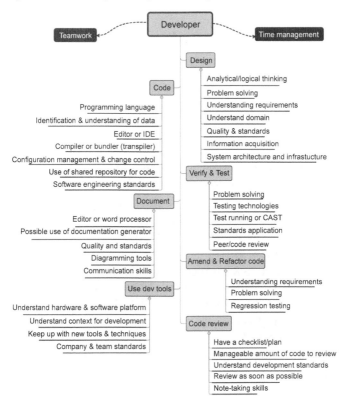

REFERENCES

Agile Alliance (2019) Details and resources for Agile. Available from www.agilealliance.org

Beck, K. et al. (2001) Manifesto for Agile Software Development. Available from http://agilemanifesto.org/

Boehm, B.W. (2014) *Incremental Commitment Spiral Model: Principles and Practices for Successful Systems and Software.* Boston, MA: Addison-Wesley Professional.

Bostian, E. (2018) How to build a captivating presentation using HTML, CSS & JavaScript. Available from https://levelup.gitconnected.com/how-to-build-a-captivating-presentation-using-html-css-javascript-a1dd0e3f1096

Crinnion, J. (1992) *Evolutionary Systems Development.* New York: Springer US.

Crockford, D. (n.d.) Introducing JSON. Available from www.json.org/

Fowler, M. with Beck, K. (2019) *Refactoring: Improving the Design of Existing Code*, 2nd edn. Reading, MA: Addison-Wesley.

Kipling, J.R. (1900) *The Elephant's Child.* The Kipling Society. Available from www.kiplingsociety.co.uk/rg_elephantschild1.htm

McConnell, S. (2004) *Code Complete*, 2nd edn. Redmond, WA: Microsoft Press.

Neon Rain (2019) Agile/Scrum for web development. Available from https://www.neonrain.com/agile-scrum-web-development/

Schwaber, K. and Sutherland, J. (2017) *The Scrum Guide.* Available from https://www.scrum.org/resources/scrum-guide

SFIA Foundation (2019) Skills and competencies version 7. Available from https://www.sfia-online.org/en/framework/sfia-7/en/framework/sfia-7/skills/solution-development-and-implementation/systems-development/programming-software-development

Stack Overflow (2019) Stack Overflow's Developer Survey 2019. Available from https://insights.stackoverflow.com/survey/2019

FURTHER READING

Albahari, J. (2017) *C# 7.0 in a Nutshell*. Sebastopol, CA: O'Reilly Media.

Allbee, B. (2018) *Hands-On Software Engineering with Python: Move beyond Basic Programming and Construct Reliable and Efficient Software with Complex Code*. Birmingham, UK: Packt Publishing.

Beaulieu, A. (2009) *Learning SQL*. Sebastopol, CA: O'Reilly Media.

Bell, D. (2005) *Software Engineering for Students: A Programming Approach* (4th edn). Reading, MA: Addison-Wesley.

Booch, G. (2017) *The Unified Modelling Language User Guide* (2nd edn). Reading, MA: Addison-Wesley.

Britton, C. and Doake, J. (2005) *Software Systems Development: A Gentle Introduction* (4th edn). Maidenhead, UK: McGraw-Hill.

Clements, A. (2006) *The Principles of Computer Hardware* (4th edn). Oxford, UK: Oxford University Press.

Cohen, J. (2006) *Best Kept Secrets of Peer Code Review*. Boston, MA: Smart Bear Inc.

Date, C.J. (2003) *An Introduction to Database Systems* (8th edn). Reading, MA: Addison-Wesley.

Deitel, H. and Deitel, P. (2016) *C How to Program* (8th edn). Harlow, UK: Prentice Hall.

Deitel, H. and Deitel, P. (2016) *Java How to Program* (10th edn). Harlow, UK: Pearson.

Deitel, H. and Deitel, P. (2018) *Python for Programmers: With Big Data and Artificial Intelligence Case Studies*. Harlow, UK: Prentice Hall.

Frain, B. (2015) *Responsive Web Design with HTML5 and CSS3* (2nd edn). Birmingham, UK: Packt Publishing.

Goodrich, M.T. and Tamassia, R. (2014) *Data Structures & Algorithms in Java* (6th edn). Hoboken, NJ: John Wiley & Sons Ltd.

Graham, I. (2000) *Object-oriented Methods* (3rd edn). Reading, MA: Addison-Wesley.

Horstmann, C.S. (2010) *Java Concepts 6/E for Java 7 and 8 International Student Version*. Hoboken, NJ: John Wiley & Sons Ltd.

Kendall, K. and Kendall, J.E. (2013) *Systems Analysis & Design* (9th edn). Harlow, UK: Prentice Hall.

Kniberg, H. (2015) *Scrum and XP from the Trenches* (2nd edn). Toronto: InfoQ.

Krug, S. (2013) *Don't Make Me Think, Revisited: A Common Sense Approach to Web Usability* (3rd edn). San Francisco, CA: New Riders.

Maciaszek, L. (2007) *Requirements Analysis and Systems Design* (3rd edn). Reading, MA: Addison-Wesley.

Martin, R.C. (2008) *Clean Code: A Handbook of Agile Software Craftsmanship*. Harlow, UK: Prentice Hall.

Metz, S. (2018) *Practical Object-Oriented Design: An Agile Primer Using Ruby*. Reading, MA: Addison-Wesley.

Nixon, R. (2018) *Learning PHP, MySQL & JavaScript 5e (Learning PHP, MYSQL, JavaScript, CSS & HTML5)*. Sebastopol, CA: O'Reilly Media.

Osmani, A. (2012) *Learning JavaScript Design Patterns*. Sebastopol, CA: O'Reilly Media.

Robertson, L.A. (2006) *Simple Program Design: A Step-By-Step Approach* (5th edn). Boston, MA: Course Technology Inc.

Savitch, W. (2009) *Problem Solving with C++* (7th edn). Harlow, UK: Pearson.

SFIA Foundation (2018) Skills and competencies version 6. Available from https://www.sfia-online.org/en/framework/sfia-6/skills/solution-development-and-implementation/systems-development/programming-software-development

Tanenbaum, A.S. (2014) *Modern Operating Systems* (4th edn). Harlow, UK: Prentice Hall.

USEFUL WEBSITES

The websites listed in this section contain information or guidance for some of the many topics covered in this book. The websites are grouped by broad category.

METHODOLOGIES AND MANAGEMENT SYSTEMS

Agile/Scrum: https://www.scrum.org/

Prince2 Agile:
https://www.axelos.com/certifications/prince2-agile

The Scrum guide:
https://www.scrum.org/resources/scrum-guide

An excellent article on CI by Martin Fowler:
https://martinfowler.com/articles/continuousIntegration.html

QUALIFICATIONS

BCS has an extensive range of qualifications and certificates:
https://www.bcs.org/get-qualified/

BCS has degree-level qualifications that will prepare you for a career in IT; for full details see the website:
https://www.bcs.org/get-qualified/international-higher-education-qualifications-heq/

TRAINING AND HELP

Stack Overflow: https://stackoverflow.com/

Free courses: www.futurelearn.com

Online courses: https://www.udemy.com/

Open source information website:
https://opensource.com/resources/what-open-source

Open source software material by The Balance Careers:
https://www.thebalancecareers.com/what-is-open-source-software-2071941

Free short course on communications skills and teamwork:
https://www.futurelearn.com/courses/categories/business-and-management-courses/communication-skills

Downloadable ebook by Microsoft on their cloud-based database
Azure: https://azure.microsoft.com/en-us/resources/microsoft-azure-options-for-sql-server-relational-databases/

Security for applications: https://www.globalknowledge.com/en-GB/Courses/Micro_Focus/Operating_Systems/FT2V0074

Half-hour video introduction to SDLCs free from Udemy:
https://www.udemy.com/sdlc-models/

Functional programming course by Mary Rose Cook:
https://maryrosecook.com/blog/post/a-practical-introduction-to-functional-programming

Nice example walkthrough of a TDD session here, it is done in
Java: https://technologyconversations.com/2013/12/20/test-driven-development-tdd-example-walkthrough/

UNIVERSITY STUDY

This is just a selection of the universities that provide qualifications in computer-related subjects.

University of East Anglia: www.uea.ac.uk/computing

University of Edinburgh: www.inf.ed.ac.uk

University of Stirling: www.stir.ac.uk/courses/?filter__level=Postgraduate,Undergraduate&query=computing

The University of Birmingham: www.cs.bham.ac.uk

University of Newcastle: www.cs.ncl.ac.uk/admissions/degrees/ug/index.php

University of Oxford: www.cs.ox.ac.uk/

Westminster: www.westminster.ac.uk/computer-science-and-software-engineering-courses

City University London: www.city.ac.uk

University of Hertfordshire: https://www.herts.ac.uk/study/schools-of-study/engineering-and-computer-science

University of Liverpool: https://www.liverpool.ac.uk/online-programmes/

DATA

UK government public data portal: https://data.gov.uk/

DIAGRAMMING

UML: www.uml.org

STANDARDS

IEEE Software Engineering Standards, the Institute of Electrical and Electronic Engineering, Inc.: https://www.computer.org

ANSI American National Standards Institute: https://www.ansi.org

ISO International Organization for Standardization: https://www.iso.org/standards.html

Accessibility advice and standards: https://www.abilitynet.org.uk/ or https://www.w3.org/WAI/intro/aria

BSI British Standards Institute: https://shop.bsigroup.com/Browse-By-Subject/ICT---Information-and-Communications-Technology-/

ISO/IEC/IEEE 25010:2011 standard: https://www.iso.org/standard/35733.html

IEEE-Std 830:1993: https://standards.ieee.org/standard/830-1998.html

CLEAN CODE AND GOOD PRACTICES

OWASP top ten: https://www.owasp.org

Dictionary of Software Weakness Types: http://cwe.mitre.org/top25

The website of Kent Beck, developer and promoter of good programming standards: https://www.kentbeck.com/

A SELECTION OF TOOLS, LIBRARIES AND APPLICATIONS FOR DEVELOPERS

PhoneGap: https://phonegap.com/about/

Sublime text (Windows, Mac, Linux):
https://www.sublimetext.com/

Visual studio code (Windows, Mac, Linux):
https://code.visualstudio.com/

Atom (Windows, Mac, Linux): https://atom.io/

Notepad++ (Windows): https://notepad-plus-plus.org/

Vim (Unix, Linux, Windows, Mac, iOS, Android, AmigaOS, MorphOS): https://www.vim.org/

Brackets (Windows, Mac, Linux, Debian): http://brackets.io/

Puppet: https://puppet.com

Git: https://git-scm.com/

Docker: https://www.docker.com/

Vagrant: https://www.vagrantup.com/

Chef: https://www.chef.io/

CAREER SUPPORT AND JOB SEARCHING

Developer report for jobs: https://hired.com/page/state-of-software-engineers/

UK government jobsite: https://mywayin.campaign.gov.uk/

Explanation of the entry requirements (for England) for apprenticeships on the UCAS page: https://www.ucas.com/alternatives/apprenticeships/apprenticeships-england/entry-requirements-apprenticeships-england

Full UCAS guide to apprenticeships: https://www.ucas.com/file/120301/download?token=DPdwJ0EV

Introduction to IT apprenticeships by Employment 4 students: https://www.e4s.co.uk/jobs/5-it-apprenticeships.htm

A site listing the professional bodies and organisations for (among others) the IT and telecommunications industry: https://directoryoftheprofessions.co.uk/it-and-telecommunications/

IET, which has some excellent resources for apprentices and other job seekers: https://www.theiet.org/career/routes-to-engineering/apprenticeships/introducing-apprenticeships/find-an-apprenticeship/

The Apprenticeship Guide: www.apprenticeshipguide.co.uk/vacancies/

The government also has an apprenticeships page: https://www.gov.uk/education/apprenticeships-traineeships-and-internships

ENDNOTES

CHAPTER 3

1. Hungarian notation – a naming standard that includes the type and intention (use) of the item being named, uses Camel Case (a mix of upper and lower case letters). For example, a counter (something you use when doing totals or sub-totals in a program) name begins with a lower case c, so that customers would be a count of customers

2. An example of a linter for JavaScript can be found here: https://jslint.com/

3. See https://www.sfia-online.org/en/framework/sfia-7/en/framework/sfia-7/skills/solution-development-and-implementation/systems-development/programming-software-development for full details.

4. Created by Ken Schwaber and Jeff Sutherland and licensed under Attribution shareAlike https://creativecommons.org/licenses/by-sa/4.0/

CHAPTER 4

1. The SOLID acronym (the acronym was created by Michael Feathers) comprises the first letters of the five principles. These are: Single responsibility principle, Open-closed principle, Liskov substitution principle, Interface segregation principle, and Dependency inversion principle.

2. Chrome has a JavaScript compiler known as V8, this compiles the JavaScript into machine code just before it runs (known as a JIT, just-in-time compiler).

3. See https://phonegap.com/about/

4. See https://electronjs.org/

5. See https://www.meteor.com/

CHAPTER 5

1. See this example on GitHub for a React-based webpage development environment: https://github.com/facebook/create-react-app

CHAPTER 6

1. https://www.bcs.org/

2. https://www.theiet.org/

3. https://hired.com/page/state-of-software-engineers/

CHAPTER 7

1. W3C refers to the World Wide Web Consortium which sets standards for web development. Accessibility compliance means ensuring that the standards for full accessibility of the application or website are met. This could include, for example, ensuring that assistive technologies such as screen readers or magnifiers work with the design.

INDEX